A Comprehensive Textbook on Biblical Preaching

PREACHING WITH PURPOSE

Jay E. Adams

Presbyterian and Reformed Publishing Company
Phillipsburg, New Jersey 08865

To
All of those preachers of the Word
who
wish
to reconsider
preaching
from
a more radically biblical
perspective.

CONTENTS

PREFACE

The work that you hold in your hands is the result of over 25 years of intensive analysis and thought about preaching. Both my doctoral degree and my master's degree were acquired in the area of preaching. Throughout the time that I taught counseling at Westminster Theological Seminary I also taught (even more) courses on preaching. Now I plan to develop, direct, and teach in a D.Min. program on preaching at the newly established western campus of Westminster Seminary in Escondido, California. It is in preparation for that program that I have finally written this book, which, in the form of notes and outlines, has been lying in a drawer of my desk for at least 12 years. My prayer is that God will use it in an effective way in the lives and ministries of many.

Jay E. Adams
The Millhouse
1982

INTRODUCTION

In my opinion, there has not appeared in the English language a significant textbook on preaching since John Broadus, a New Testament scholar, wrote his landmark book, *The Preparation and Delivery of Sermons.* I make that statement advisedly after studying and teaching preaching intensively for over 25 years. Many good books on preaching have been published. Each is helpful in its own way, but none has done for contemporary preachers what Broadus did for his fellow ministers in his day.

"Perhaps Broadus' work was enough; why attempt to move ahead of him?" someone may wonder. I only wish that were the case. If it were, it would save us all a great amount of anguish and effort, and instead of writing this book I could devote my time to other tasks. But it isn't. Broadus' approach, his style, etc., were helpful to those who were called to preach in another era, not like our own. He codified for his generation, and the one that followed, much of the best that had been said thus far. But his approach to preaching hardly begins to meet the problems ministers must face today, and certainly not in a form that is pertinent to the contemporary scene.

Moreover, in all candor it must be said that, like those who preceded him, and many who have followed, Broadus by-passed a number of important matters and, at the same time, retained much of the scholastic approach, which has served to weaken rather than strengthen the preaching of those who have adopted it. Scholasticism, Rome's dubious legacy to Protestantism, was mediated to us through the English Puritans, who took a number of wrong turns in preaching—some of which have brought us to the present sorry plight in which the evangelical church finds itself.

That last statement points up a major reason why I have been impelled to assume the task that has produced this book. My goal has been to develop a textbook on preaching for pastors, seminary students, and other Christian speakers that, I hope, will make an impact in our day significant enough to change preaching substantially.

That, with few—and I mean *very* few—notable exceptions, preachers need to change what they are doing is not a point that I shall argue. If you are of the mind that, on the whole, preaching in America is tolerably good (or, for that matter, even tolerable), then you and I are on such entirely different wavelengths that I don't think I could convince you to see it otherwise, no matter how hard I tried. So I won't. But if you are among those who recognize the great deficiencies that exist and would like to do something significant about the situation, even if it might mean taking radical departures from your present practices, then I believe this is the book for you. This book is not a mere restatement of past ideas and practices in contemporary language. It takes a new turn.

As there was a need for a definitive change in Christian counseling when I wrote *Competent to Counsel,* so too is there a need for such change in *all* areas of the practical field—in administration, Christian education,[1] pastoral work—but *especially* in preaching. I have been a consumer of thousands of sermons in my lifetime—far more than the average person, since at seminary I often listened to well over a hundred sermons each semester—and while I must say I have heard

---

1. In another book, aimed at foundationally changing Christian education, I have attempted to do the same thing. That book is *Back to the Blackboard* (Phillipsburg, N.J.: Presbyterian and Reformed Publishing Co., 1982).

some good preaching, in all honesty I must say also that there has been much, much more poor preaching. My experience has not been isolated to novices, however; I have heard conference speakers, seminary professors, pastors, and just about every other sort of preacher there is, from every sort of background and denomination. Yet the story is the same: poor preaching predominates. Everywhere I go I hear the same complaint from laymen: "Why don't the seminaries teach men to preach?" The question is not just a part of the typical griping that goes on all the time; it has a solid basis in fact. And it is asked most frequently by those who are most sincere in their faith, not as an excuse to cover irresponsible behavior, but as a genuine, heartfelt cry. Men and women (and especially young people) are being turned away from Christ and His church by dull, unarresting, unedifying, and aimless preaching. The question about seminaries is a legitimate and live one.

"Well, why *don't* the seminaries do a better job?"

That question haunts homiletics departments everywhere. Part of the answer will be found in the inadequate structure of seminaries themselves, part in the failure of the church leadership to take the matter of ministerial selection and ordination more seriously, and part in the almost unbelievable willingness of congregations to put up with mediocrity or worse.

At any rate, the present crisis in preaching need not, indeed *must* not, be permitted to continue. Something must be done about the situation. While I do not expect to see great changes in the structure of theological education in the near future (there are too many persons with too many vested interests of various sorts who are too deeply entrenched for that), there is one place from which I think I can realistically hope for change—from faithful, concerned pastors and seminary students. And, because homiletic professors in particular, as well as practical theology professors in general, are so often considered a breed apart by other teachers in the seminary, there is hope that they too may find it easier to break the chains of tradition that so tightly bind most other theological academes.

Over the last few years I have had the opportunity to work with thousands of Bible-believing preachers and theological students both in this country and abroad. While there are numerous exceptions, of course, I find them to be an overwhelmingly genuine group of men. They are anxious to please Christ, willing to listen to new ideas and approaches (provided they can be shown to be biblical), and dedicated to personal improvement. As a whole, they seem far more acclimated to change than do their counterparts in educational and administrative posts. They have been the hapless recipients of an education that they, by bitter experience, have learned is deficient in any number of ways and that, as a result, has failed to equip them for their ministerial tasks. They are embarrassed and hurt, and find themselves scrambling for whatever help they can get (just look at all the pastors' conferences they attend!).

These pastors have experienced the problems one faces on the battlefronts of Christian ministry. They know that, in many cases, they were required to spend inordinate amounts of time studying what now seems to have been the esoteric interests of professors who, themselves, at this point in their careers are so far removed from the battlefield (if they were ever on it at all) that they are out of touch with the pastor's needs. Sometimes, from the abstract, "scholarly" and "academic" ways in which these instructors run their recruits through basic training, one wonders whether they have not lost sight of the fact that they are there to train good soldiers of Jesus Christ rather than more trainers like themselves. Too often teachers require of students what should be required only of those who, themselves, will become teachers. Of course, I do not wish to make a wholesale indictment; there are great, notable exceptions to what, sad to say, is the *rule*.

This is no place to discuss all of the reasons for the failure of the theological seminary to train good preachers. Part of the problem, as I said, is conceptual and structural, part pertains to curriculum, part is a matter of content, and part is rooted in methodology. Elsewhere I have set forth a plan for theological education that is designed to solve these and other problems.[2] Nor shall I discuss the church's failure to

2. See my article, "Design for a Theological Seminary," in *The Journal of Pastoral Practice* 3, 2 (1979): 1. All issues of this journal are available and may be

properly recruit, select, and nurture students for ministerial training (I have also addressed that vital issue in "Design"—see footnote 2, *supra*).

My present desire is to do whatever I can to help the average preacher who is out there on the front line, struggling daily because, as he knows all too well, his training and resources have proved woefully inadequate for the task. He longs for help; he buys and devours every new volume on preaching that appears; he attends pastors' conferences, but he finds little that is new and virtually nothing that will make any significant changes in his preaching. Such men are hungry for something to sink their teeth into. One pastor at such a conference (every time he passed me in the hall) said, "Please write that book on preaching!" While pastors (and congregations) have proved that they can survive on bread and water, they deserve something more nutritional. It is for these men and their congregations especially that this book has been written.[3]

Preaching with Purpose may be used by an individual or in a class. The class assignments at the conclusion of chapters are designed for teachers to use in formal situations, but individual readers also may wish to adapt them for their own personal benefit.

My hope is that this textbook on preaching may be even more influential in its area than *Competent to Counsel* has been in counseling. There is every bit as great a need for a change in preaching as there was in counseling.

---

obtained by writing to C.C.E.F., 1790 E. Willow Grove, Laverock, PA 19118. This article also is reprinted in the appendix of my book on Christian education, *Back to the Blackboard*.

3. Of course, some homiletics professors will welcome the text. Students in seminary, on the whole, do not know the problems in the pastorate and are inclined to discount practical theology for "the real courses." Later, they find themselves among the starved.

Class Assignments:

1. Interview at least five pastors. Ask them about their training in homiletics. Find out if they think it was adequate, what they have done to supplement it and whether they would even now welcome help in preaching. Ask if they have read this book and if they have followed its teaching. If so, find out if they think that doing so has helped their preaching.
2. Write out a paragraph expressing your current ideas concerning the purpose and place of preaching. Be ready to discuss this topic in class.

1

THE CENTRALITY
OF PURPOSE

"Why the title of this book—*Preaching with Purpose?* Why a book on this subject at all?" There are reasons, good reasons. Let me mention several.

First, there is a need to examine and to stress purpose because there is so much purposeless preaching today in which the preacher has only the vaguest idea of what he wants to achieve. The members of congregations who are subjected to this sort of preaching for any length of time, as a result, both individually and corporately, themselves, become aimless and confused.

Secondly, the amazing lack of concern for purpose among homileticians and preachers has spawned a brood of preachers who are dull, lifeless, abstract, and impersonal; it has obscured truth, hindered joyous Christian living, destroyed dedication and initiative, and stifled service for Christ. But of greatest concern in my choice of the title for this book is a basic consideration that lies behind all others: I am convinced that purpose is of such vital importance to all a preacher does that it ought to control his thinking and actions from start to finish in the preparation and delivery of sermons. It is my purpose in this book, therefore, to make the reader aware of this all-important role of purpose in preaching and to demonstrate to him that he must be aware of it from now on in all of his preaching endeavors. That is how basic purpose is.

Yet, so unaware of the centrality of purpose is the average homiletician that you can hardly find a discussion of the subject in homiletics textbooks, let alone discover a book in which purpose is set forth as the central or controlling factor in preaching. This lack of concern about purpose, along with an emphasis on competing concerns about "central ideas," "themes," "topics," "subjects," etc., that deflect one's thinking into wrong channels and debase preaching to little more than a lecture instead of the life-transforming experience that God intended it to be, is at the bottom of the problems in preaching to which I referred in the introduction. And, even in those rare instances in which the preacher becomes aware of the role of purpose in preaching, so often the purpose he adopts is his own purpose rather than the purpose of the Holy Spirit underlying the biblical preaching portion. This sad state of affairs must be remedied if we would enter a new era in preaching. Our thinking about preaching, along with our methods of preparation and delivery, needs a complete overhaul. More is in order than the usual oil-change-and-grease-job that the average book on preaching offers.

Even when discussing such narrow questions as, "Should I announce my points to the congregation?" and, "Is there a need for an illustration here?" a focus on purpose is altogether essential to reach more than the usual unsatisfying, arbitrary answers. In response to those questions, a third—a purpose question—also must be asked: "What would be the purpose of announcing your points?" or, "What purpose would an illustration serve here?" Purpose, as you can see, gets back behind the surface discussions to fundamental issues— something that we have largely failed to do in the teaching and practice of preaching.

My reason for focusing on purpose, then, is to show its basic and central place in preaching. It is only when we purposefully make the requisite changes that a transformation in preaching can occur.

Purpose is the central issue. The preacher's purpose in preaching, the purpose of the text, the purpose of the sermon content, of the organization, of the style, of the illustrative materials, of the type of delivery used—all of these and much more are crucial to good preaching. Yet, ask the average preacher, "What purpose did you have in mind when you used that example?" and he may be hard-put to tell you. Ask him, "What was your purpose in presenting the material in that order?" and he may be at a loss to respond. Indeed, ask some preachers, "What was the purpose of that sermon?" and they will reply, "What do you mean, 'What was the purpose' of my sermon? My purpose was to preach, of course. It was Sunday morning, and I am paid to hold forth every Sunday morning—in case you don't realize it!" Of course, few would put it quite so crassly; surely *you* wouldn't! But, ask yourself, how often have you not found yourself doing just that—preaching because it is expected of you, because the time to preach had rolled around once again? Whether you realize it or not, when you did so your basic purpose was to fill a slot in a weekly service allotted to preaching; your purpose was to "do your duty," to fulfil your contract. While the fulfillment of a contract is a worthy purpose, it certainly is not an adequate one for preaching. Pastor, what is your purpose in preaching?

Or, take a different sort of question: Why did you use the illustration that you used under point III-A-1 in your sermon last week? That is to say, what was your purpose in using it? Did you use it because it was the first to come to mind? Did you select it from among a number of others because its tone, as well as its thrust, seemed appropriate to what you were trying to say? And, for that matter, what was your purpose in using an illustration in that part of the sermon? Did you think that it was about time for another illustration? Did you believe a truth needed to be clarified? Was it necessary to emphasize, particularize, show how to implement and/or integrate some truth into life?—or what?

All of these questions about purpose, not to mention hundreds of others that might have been asked, are getting at one thing: *Whatever you do in a sermon, you should do consciously and deliberately to achieve some purpose.* In other words, everything should have its objective, and you ought to know what that is. That is to say, just as you expect an automobile mechanic to know the purpose of every part of your car, and just as you expect him to have a clear and correct purpose in every adjustment or repair that he makes, so too should your congregation expect at least as much of you. After all, you are not tinkering with automobiles; your preaching will affect lives, for good or for ill—for eternity. How much more important it is, then, for you to be a craftsman, well informed about and skilled in the work of preaching—"a workman who won't be ashamed!" (II Tim. 2:15).

Because it is vital for you to plan and execute everything that you do in preaching according to a well-understood, clearly articulated, and biblically justifiable purpose, you must be willing to consider all of preaching from the point of view of purpose. I know of no better way to think basically about preaching. Therefore, I shall lead you through the field of preaching, stopping here and there to ask, in one way or another, "What purpose does this serve?" And we shall settle for nothing less than biblical and biblically derived answers.

As that question is posed again and again in every sort of context, I trust you will become more and more concerned about the *rationale* for doing whatever you do in preaching. And as I attempt to give fundamental replies, I trust that these will orient you correctly and will give you such a thorough and basic understanding of preaching that you will be in a position to evaluate and improve upon your preaching for the rest of your ministry.

Class Assignments:

1. Make a list of at least 25 practices commonly associated with preaching. Ask of each, "What is the purpose for this?" and next to it write your answer. Bring these to class to discuss.
2. Determine how many of the 25 (if any) cannot be said to be grounded on a biblical base.

2

WHAT IS PREACHING?

Strictly speaking, the principal biblical words translated "preaching" do not correspond exactly to that activity to which we affix the label. They are somewhat narrower in scope. These words, *kerusso* and *euangelizo*, are used in the New Testament to describe "heralding" and "announcing the gospel." They refer to evangelistic activity. The former always has to do with public proclamation of the good news, while the latter may be used to describe making the gospel known to either unsaved groups or individuals (cf. Acts 8:35). On the other hand, the word *didasko*, translated "to teach," more nearly corresponds to our modern use of the word preach,[1] and has to do with the proclamation of truth among those who already believe the gospel (cf. I Cor. 4:17).

This distinction follows naturally from the background of two of the words. The Greek city-state was composed of three classes: citizens (a distinct minority), slaves, and freedmen (the latter two classes constituting the vast majority of the population). Whenever

---

1. Though at times *didasko* seems also to be limited to evangelistic speaking, and occasionally it is possible that *kerusso* may refer to preaching to the saints (cf. II Tim. 4:2).

5

there was a vote to be taken, or the citizens were required to assemble for some other purpose, the *kerux* ("herald") went about the streets of the city proclaiming the fact. As he did, he summoned the citizens to come out from among the total population so that this *ekklesia* ("assembly" or "church") of "called out ones" might gather to transact the business of the city. Similarly, God's heralds of the gospel go about preaching the good news, and those persons who respond in faith assemble as God's *ekklesia* ("church" or "called out ones") to transact God's business as citizens of His heavenly kingdom. They are called *out* of the world and called *to be* "saints." Heralding the gospel (*kerusso*), then, is an evangelistic enterprise just as surely as is "announcing the good news" (*euangelizo*, the word from which our word "evangelize" comes).

Whatever speaking is carried on in the church after it has assembled, though never divorced from the gospel message, is *didaskalia*, or "teaching" (cf. I Tim. 4:16; 5:17). It also may be called simply "speaking" (*lalia*) as it is in I Corinthians 1:6. Both *didaskalia* and *lalia*, among other things, include *paraklesis* ("aid, assistance, advice, exhortation, encouragement, urging"), *paramuthia* ("comfort, cheer"), and *nouthesia* ("counsel, admonition") as well as instruction (cf. Titus 2:15).

There are, then, two kinds of preaching (because of a deeply impressed use of the English word I shall use the term "preaching" to cover both evangelistic and pastoral speaking): evangelistic preaching (heralding, announcing the good news) and pastoral or edificational preaching (teaching). While I shall try to distinguish between the two often enough to make it perfectly clear in any context what I am talking about, I also shall use simply the words "preaching" and "preacher" for either activity, whenever there is no doubt about which activity is in view. Because this book more largely treats pastoral preaching ("teaching to observe"—Matt. 28:20), I shall most frequently have that in mind when using the word "preaching" without any other qualification.

There are several elements in preaching (of both sorts) that may be distinguished. Phillips Brooks defined preaching as "truth through personality." In that definition he distinguished two elements: *truth* (which we must modify to read "divine truth" or "God's truth") and *personality* (the preacher). But, as elegant as Brooks's definition may be, it surely must be rejected as inadequate. For one thing, it fails to mention the *occasion,* which at times (e.g., on the day of Pentecost, when Peter preached) may be important. And of greater significance, it says nothing of the *audience* or congregation (too often preachers have prepared and preached sermons that had little relevance to those who came to hear). But the greatest deficiency of all is Brooks's failure to include the presence and work of the *Holy Spirit,* apart from whom preaching is worthless, indeed, injurious. So then, preaching necessarily involves:

1. Content, in the form of a biblical message;
2. A preacher;
3. An occasion (in which I include time and place);
4. Listeners;
5. The Holy Spirit.

A proper understanding of and attitude toward preaching always requires the proper purposeful relationship of each of these five elements to the other four. Whenever any one or more of them is neglected, ignored, or is otherwise out of sync with the rest, problems arise.

Of all, of course, the fifth element is most essential. When He wishes to do so, the Holy Spirit may bless our preaching in spite of poorly exegeted and constructed messages, even when given through preachers whose lives are out of tune with the revealed will of God (cf. Phil. 1:15-18), in seemingly inauspicious circumstances (II Tim. 4:2), and in the lives of persons dead in trespasses and sins.

"Why then," you ask, "should we concern ourselves about the other four elements? If, after all is said and done, the Holy Spirit is the operative factor in preaching, aren't the other elements merely window-dressing and actually non-functional?"

No. Absolutely not. While it is essential for successful preaching (i.e., preaching that meets God's requirements all around, regardless of visible results), to have the blessing of the Spirit at work in both the preacher and the listener, it is the *message, delivered* to an *audience* by the *preacher,* on a particular *occasion* that *He* uses to bring about that blessing. He does not bless in the abstract; He has chosen to use means. And, while the Holy Spirit, on occasion, may bless in spite of failures at any point, ordinarily He does not do so.[2] He puts no premium on sloppy efforts. Regardless of what the Spirit determines to do, when and where and how He pleases, He requires the best of a preacher, to whom He says,

> Do your best to present yourself to God tried and true, a workman who won't be ashamed, rightly handling the Word of truth with accuracy (II Tim. 2:15).

Clearly, God will hold preachers responsible for doing a good job as workmen in the Word. That is one reason "preaching and teaching" are viewed as laborious activities, and why God tells His church to pay double wages to those who do a good job (I Tim. 5:17, 18[3]). That is also why the Holy Spirit instructs the preacher to "pay attention to yourself and to your teaching" (I Tim. 3:2) and why He limits the office to those who are "competent to teach others" (II Tim. 2:2) and "able to teach" (I Tim. 3:2). It is also why He warns them, "Let each one watch how he builds" (I Cor. 3:10[b]).

"All that may be well and good, but," you may yet protest, "I didn't think that preachers are supposed to try to become orators. Surely books and courses on preaching are unnecessary if oratory isn't what God wants. Paul certainly didn't seem enamored with oratory when he wrote, 'And I did not deliver my message or preach in persuasive words of wisdom, but with proof and power provided by the Spirit, so that you might not place your faith in human wisdom,

---

2. Ian Maclaren wrote: ". . . believing that as the blessing of the Divine Spirit will only rest on the outcome of hard, honest work, the more thorough and skillful that work is, the more likely is it to be crowned with prosperity." *The Cure of Souls* (New York: Dodd, Mead & Co., 1896), p. 8.

3. "The elders who manage well should be considered worthy of double pay, especially those who are laboring at preaching and teaching. The Scripture says, 'Do not muzzle the ox while he is treading out the grain,' and 'The worker is worthy of his wages.' "

but rather in God's power' (I Cor. 2:4, 5), did he? Why, then, should I study preaching?''

What Paul was conscientious to avoid was the bag of rhetorical tricks and gimmicks used by the Greek sophists—the same sort of thing that Socrates rejected with disdain in Plato's *Apology* (see, e.g., II Cor. 2:17; 4:2; I Thess. 2:3, 5). Moreover, you are right in supposing that Paul was not interested in oratory. He cared nothing about praise for his brilliant speech. Rather, his great concern was to make the message as clear as possible (Col. 4:3, 4). He wanted to be sure that he did not obscure it (I Cor. 2:2, 3) and that the faith of those who believed rested on the proper foundation (I Cor. 2:5; 3:11). And that also is exactly what any correct instruction in homiletics ought to be all about—learning

1. how to remove all obstacles to preaching the truth;
2. how to make the message as clear as possible;
3. how to point the listener to Christ alone as the foundation for his belief and actions.

Books and courses in homiletics that stress oratory and eloquence err. Throughout this volume I shall attempt instead to do the above three things. My purpose is to help you become a more faithful and more effective preacher of the Word so that men will not praise you for your speaking ability, but will praise only the Christ whom you preach.

It is because of that purpose that I am taking you on an excursion into the fundamentals of preaching from the perspective of purpose. The emphasis on purpose itself will tend to lead us away from the many superficial and trivial matters that so often find their way into books on preaching. Our focus throughout will be on the basics.[4]

4. In this book I have omitted many matters often included in homiletics books, not because they all were wrong or useless, but because, in reflecting on basic questions that have been neglected, I do not want to stray into by-paths.

Class Assignments:

1. Study the use of the word *euangelizo, kerusso,* or *laleo* in relationship to preaching in all its occurrences in the New Testament and summarize your findings, illustrating each point by concrete examples. Write out a report to be handed in or given orally.
2. Study the use of *didasko* in relationship to Christ's preaching. Be ready to discuss your findings in class.

THE PURPOSE
OF PREACHING

What is the purpose of pastoral preaching—why should a pastor preach? Why did God ordain that this activity should be carried on in His church? A proper answer to the second question must be the same as the correct answer to the first. Unfortunately, in the minds of many pastors these answers do not always closely correspond to one another.

Surely a preacher must not preach merely to fulfil a weekly obligation. That his task involves such an obligation is plain, and for him to want to fulfil that obligation faithfully is neither wrong nor unimportant. But it isn't enough, and it isn't basic enough. He must know what is required of him when he arrives on the scene to preach. Even before that, he must know what he must achieve when he plans and prepares in his study. He must know what God expects him to do if he is ever to accomplish it. In short, he must know plainly what the purpose of pastoral preaching is.

The people of God come together by God's command (Heb. 10:25[1]) on the first day of the week not only for fellowship or mutual

1. "We must not abandon our practice of meeting together, as some are in the habit of doing, but rather, we must encourage each other, and all the more as you see the day drawing near."

11

encouragement, counseling, and admonition, but also to hear the explanation and application of the Word from those who "labor at preaching and teaching" (I Tim. 5:17). There is a preaching task in view. To achieve these purposes—the explanation and application of Scripture—God ordained regular preaching in His church. That is why a preacher should preach. But what is the essence of *a faithful* fulfillment of that task? That is the question.

The pastoral preacher must be prepared at each gathering of the saints to use the Word in some way in order to "equip" them for their work of ministry. That is paramount. To honor God (the ultimate objective of all that a believer does), the preacher's purpose must be God's purpose. There can be no doubt that the pastoral preacher is obligated to meet that need: "And He gave some as apostles, some as prophets, some as evangelists and some as shepherds and teachers, to equip the saints for a work of service leading to the building up of Christ's body" (Eph. 4:11, 12). Pastoral preaching is a prime means for doing so. Faithful fulfillment of his weekly task, then, entails *edificational* preaching. The minister of the Word is a mason who goes to church each week to lay block. He builds on a foundation, and to be faithful he must build that which will be able to withstand the fires of testing (I Cor. 3:10-15).

This obligation to build is met, in part, in the weekly assembly, when the "whole church" of God's people "comes together" in order to "meet together" (I Cor. 11:20; 14:23, 26). According to I Corinthians 14:3, the specifically stated body-building *purposes* of preaching are "edification" itself (i.e., the building up of the body and each of its parts), "assistance" (*paraklesis* = standing by another to offer whatever aid necessary) and "encouragement" (*paramuthia* = comfort, cheer). [2] But, because the word "edification" runs through-

---

2. Notice, the *fundamental* purposes of teaching *in the assembly* do not include evangelism. That conversions, nevertheless, may occur under such preaching is understood (cf. I Cor. 14:24, 25). That is because pastoral preaching relates everything to the redemptive work of Christ; the gospel is in every message. But evangelism proper is to be carried on *outside the assembly*. In Acts, a treatise on evangelism, no one is said to be converted in a Christian assembly.

out the chapter (and elswhere) as a summary term, seemingly including the other two, I also shall use it broadly to include all that is envisioned in the New Testament as the goal of pastoral preaching.

The purpose of preaching, then, is to effect *changes* among the members of God's church that build them up individually and that build up the body as a whole. *Individually,* good pastoral preaching helps each person in the congregation to grow in his faith, conforming his life more and more to biblical standards. *Corporately,* such preaching builds up the church as a body in the relationship of the parts to the whole, and the whole to God and to the world. The important fact to grasp here—a fact too often overlooked in any such discussions—is that in the Bible edification is viewed both as an individual and as a corporate matter: individuals must be "edified" (Rom. 14:19; I Thess. 5:11), and the church as an entity must be "edified" (Eph. 4:11-16; I Cor. 14:4, 5, 17, 26). Therefore, both the pastor who ignores the forest for the trees and the one who neglects the trees for the forest err. They must always have both concerns in view. Their sermons certainly must focus on individual change, but not for the sake of the individual alone; how that change honors God by blessing the whole is equally important. Likewise, their sermons may address congregational concerns, but not in ways that would by-pass individual responsibility. In order to "build up," both the command to love God and the command to love one's neighbor must be held up. An either/or approach to pastoral preaching (except as a step toward a both/and result) is always unscriptural and therefore deficient.

Probably today there is much less emphasis on the corporate aspects of edification (the upbuilding of the entire body, as body) than there ought to be. In America, at least, we still wade around in the foam of a mighty wave of "rugged individualism," as it has been called. It is possible, however, that the tide is beginning to turn and that in the near future we may find ourselves drenched by an emphasis on corporate responsibility that is of tidal wave proportions. It is the preacher's task to keep a careful watch on the sea, not that he may go surfing on whatever waves come rolling in, but rather that he may

maintain a good balance in spite of (and often in the face of) current
surges that threaten to engulf his congregation.

Building the Church

The admonition, "... be sure that everything builds up" (I Cor.
14:26), has to do with all of those activities that are carried on in the
assembly of God's people, including the preaching of the Word.[3] But
how is the church "built up," individually and corporately? The
answer that the Bible gives everywhere is through the teaching of
truth.

Jesus set forth the edificational program for His church immediately before His ascension when He said, "teaching them to observe
all that I have commanded you" (Matt. 28:20). Those commandments are all recorded in the Scriptures. They are of two sorts:

1. Commands that build up love for God;
2. Commands that build up love for neighbors.[4]

Roughly speaking, these two commandments, which embrace all
others, correspond to (1) the edification of the *individual* and (2) the
edification of the *body*. In them is "all" that Christ commanded. So,
then, in order to discover what teaching builds up the church, one
must locate and understand all that Christ commanded. These commands, of course, may be found not only in the Gospels, but also in
the God-breathed Epistles and in the rest of the New Testament as
well.

It is precisely that sort of teaching that we find in the Scriptures
themselves. In the Epistles (cf. Rom. 12:14-21 with Matt. 5:39, 44,
for instance) we see the apostles both making their readers aware of
what Christ taught ("teaching") and pressing these commands on
them ("to observe"). Note carefully the twofold thrust of Christ's

3. Note that in I Cor. 14:26 "teaching" is specifically mentioned.
4. "And He replied, 'You must love the Lord your God with all your heart and
with all your soul and with all your mind. This is the great and first commandment.
The second is just like it: You must love your neighbor as yourself. On those two
commandments hang all the Law and the Prophets.' "

words: (1) "teaching" (2) "to observe." It is not the naked proclamation of truth that He had in view but rather *truth translated into life*. Accordingly, in the pastoral letters, (I, II Timothy and Titus) the key word of command is "teach." Yet, it is clear that along with instruction about facts, "truth" is given in order to promote "godliness" (Titus 1:1). That is why such words as "urge," "reprove," "rebuke," "insist," "encourage," "appeal," etc., also appear in these letters as apostolic injunctions to preachers. These terms have to do with *observance* of commands. To "observe" is to keep Christ's commands and transform His truth into godly living and ministry. Both as individuals and as a body this must take place. Together, then, truth observed is the goal or purpose of pastoral preaching. In order to be faithful to his task, therefore, the pastoral preacher must know not only the truth but how to communicate it effectively. Again, he must learn not only how truth should affect life but how to help his listeners knead that truth into life—individually and corporately lived.

Class Assignments:

1. From biblical study determine 20 ways that a congregation might need to be edified and
2. Decide how you might do so by preaching.
3. Be prepared to discuss these in class.

THE PURPOSE OF BIBLICAL PREACHING

What is the purpose of preaching from a scriptural passage? Why not just preach? The apostles didn't always use a text; why should we? Is this some pious practice, arbitrarily developed in the course of church history?

First of all, we must recognize that the apostles were the recipients and the earthly source of special revelation; indeed, they themselves were writing Scripture! We are not. That makes quite a difference. Moreover, we have no record of an apostolic address given in a Christian assembly. But we do see Jesus, "as was His custom," entering the synagogue and preaching from the biblical portion assigned for the day:

> Then He went to Nazareth, where He had been brought up, and, as was His custom, He went to the synagogue on the Sabbath day. The book by Isaiah the prophet was handed to Him. He opened the book and found the place where it was written, "The Lord's Spirit is on Me because He anointed Me to announce the good news to the poor. He has sent me to preach release to the captives and recovery of sight to the blind, to set free those who are downtrodden, to preach the Lord's year of favor." Then He closed the book, returned it to the attendant and sat down. The

eyes of everybody in the synagogue were fixed on Him. Then He began to speak to them: "Today this Scripture has been fulfilled in your hearing." And everybody spoke well about Him, and they were surprised at what gracious words came from His mouth. And they said, "Isn't this Joseph's son?" And He said to them, "Doubtless you will quote this proverb: 'Physician, heal yourself; do here in your home town the same things that we have heard you did at Capernaum.' " And He continued, "Let Me assure you that no prophet is accepted in his home town. As a matter of fact, I tell you, there were many widows in Israel in the days of Elijah when the sky was shut up for three and a half years and there was a great famine over the whole land. Elijah wasn't sent to any of them but only to a widow in Zarepta, in the land of Sidon. And there were many lepers in Israel in the time of the prophet Elisha, yet not a single one of them was cleansed, except Naaman the Syrian." When they heard this they were all filled with rage and rose up and threw Him out of the city, and led Him to the brow of the hill on which their city was built, in order to throw Him over. But He passed through the midst of them and left.

He went down to Capernaum, a city of Galilee. And He taught them every Sabbath. They were surprised at His teaching, because what He said had authority (Luke 4:16-32).

In the synagogue there was a reading desk or raised platform in the center. The teacher stood to read and then sat to teach. That is what Jesus did. This teaching consisted of exposition of the portion read, and exhortation growing out of it.[1] When Jesus taught in the synagogue, therefore, He clearly identified Himself with synagogue teaching forms and structures. So when the Christian assemblies began to meet, they too carried on the same practices. This is what they must have understood Jesus to mean, at least in part, when He ordered His followers to "teach" converts "to observe" His commandments:

And Jesus went to them and said to them, "All authority in heaven and on earth has been given to Me. Go, therefore, and make disciples from all nations, baptizing them into the Name of

---

1. But, according to Acts 13:15ff., 27, other topics could be addressed.

the Father and of the Son and of the Holy Spirit, teaching them to observe all that I have commanded you; and remember, I will be with you always, to the close of the age'' (Matt. 28:18-20).

They could have understood Jesus' order ''to teach'' in no other way; this is the way He taught in assemblies, so this is how they taught. The identity between the synagogue and the Christian assembly was so close that James even called the latter a ''synagogue'' (James 2:2). Who else would provide the teaching model for Christian gatherings if it were not Jesus, whose favorite title for Himself was ''teacher''?

There seems to be a reference to this teaching format inherited from the synagogue in I Timothy 4:13, where it is stated that it is a part of the pastor's task to read the Scriptures publicly, to teach what the Scriptures mean, and to exhort the congregation to follow the teaching.

The most fundamental purpose in preaching from a Scripture portion is to obey Jesus and follow His example. Today we can ''teach'' Christians to ''observe all'' that Jesus ''commanded'' only by turning to the pages of the New Testament on which those commandments are found. So, again, as in Old Testament times, we must turn to the Scriptures as the sole source of what we teach. And, according to synagogue practice, Jesus' example, His order to teach all He commanded, and the task of the pastor recorded in I Timothy 4:3, we must publicly[2] read a portion of the Scriptures, explain its meaning, and apply it to the congregation. The *basic* current practice in Bible-believing churches is fundamentally correct in these respects, but the way in which it is pursued often leaves much to be desired.

The purpose for grounding one's teaching on the Scriptures is also clear: the passage from which you preach serves as your authoritative source of truth. The authority of the apostles was in their apostolic commission; it had to be—the New Testament had not yet been written. They could speak, at times, without basing their remarks on the Bible. That was not only because the apostles were the recipients

2. That is what the word in I Tim. 4:31 means: ''public reading.''

of special revelation but also because they were given a unique ability to infallibly recall what Jesus had said (John 15:26; 16:4) and could preach from His oral teachings even though those teachings had not yet been codified in the Gospels. We are not apostles, and the promises in John 15 and 16 are not for us, but we can preach from the same source because the apostles and prophets not only taught truth orally, but they have given us Christ's teaching in the New Testament books (cf. II Thess. 2:15). Like them, we too base our teaching on the same authoritative source: God's Word. So, like them, we too can preach with authority. For them, that Word (given after the Old Testament writings) was oral; for us, it is written. But both alike are God's inerrant Word. It is in obedience to God's command, therefore, to "preach the Word" (II Tim. 4:2) that we preach what is in the Bible. Today we have no Word to preach other than the inspired written record of that Word that the apostles preached. To be sure of the apostolicity of what we say, we must ground all of our teaching on the written Word.

Preachers today have no authority for preaching their own notions and opinions; they must "preach the Word"—the apostolic Word recorded in the Scriptures. Whenever preachers depart from the purpose and the intent of a biblical portion, to that extent they lose their authority to preach. In short, the purpose of reading, explaining, and applying a portion of Scripture is to obey the command to "preach the Word." In no other way may we expect to experience the presence and power of the Holy Spirit in our preaching. He did not spend thousands of years producing the Old and New Testaments (in a sense, the Bible is peculiarly *His* Book) only to ignore it! What He "moved" men to write[3] He now motivates us to preach. He has not promised to bless our word; that promise extends only to His own (Isa.55:10, 11). Since, as we have seen already, there is no genuine

---

3. II Peter 1:16-21 makes it clear that the "prophetic Word" is more solid than experience because it was inerrantly inspired by the Holy Spirit, who "carried along" the speaker-writers as they revealed His prophecies to men. That is why he bids us to "pay attention" to it "as to a lamp shining in a dismal place" (v. 19). The Word was embodied in Scripture for pastoral teachers of all ages to be able to do so.

preaching where the Spirit of God is not at work (He is the one who changes the lives of His people; that change is called the "fruit"— that is, the *result* of the work—of the *Spirit*), we may say that the fundamental purpose behind preaching from the Bible is simply that, in any genuine sense of the word, we may preach at all!

Thus, the purposes of preaching from a Scripture portion may be summarized as follows:

1. To obey God;
2. To preach with authority;
3. To preach with power;
4. To preach effectively;
5. To preach at all!

Class Assignment:

Make an exegetical and historical study of Christ's use of a Scripture passage in Luke 4:15ff. Write up your conclusions about the matter in a five- to ten-page paper.

DETERMINING THE PREACHING PORTION

But how do you know what Scripture to choose for a sermon? And, even if you can decide upon a general area, how do you determine how much of that area to use as a preaching portion? Again, the answer lies in purpose.

"Do I begin with the preaching portion or the congregation?"

The answer to that very important question is that you must begin with *both,* but with an emphasis on the congregation. If you are selecting individual Scripture portions that are not in succession—a very legitimate way to preach when done properly—then you must always have the congregation in mind. You do not merely preach about whatever may happen to intrigue you. That is not a legitimate purpose in preaching.[1] Remember, your purpose is to honor God by *building up* His church. It is their needs, failures, opportunities, etc., that should impel you to choose as you do each week. Your purpose in preaching is to edify the flock.

1. But, of course, the study of a passage of Scripture itself may alert you to a congregational need; indeed, there is no other way to determine what congregational needs are than by discovering them in the Scriptures. A good place to begin studying is Rev. 2, 3.

On the other hand, if you are preaching consecutively through a Bible book, or through a long section (e.g., the Sermon on the Mount), then you do not make weekly selections (though you will have to determine how much you will consider each week of what remains); the very course that you have set for yourself determines that. Yet, even here you should keep in mind that when you originally selected this long section or book, your selection should have been made on the basis of the congregation's needs.

There is a seemingly "pious" approach that says "I'll take a book and, in that way, let God tell me what to preach." Fine. There is certainly nothing wrong with preaching through Bible books; indeed, there are quite a few advantages in doing so. Probably this way of preaching ought to comprise the bulk of one's preaching. But it is no more "pious" or "spiritual" to use that method than to select, on your own, a new preaching portion for each sermon. After all, who selects the Bible book? Some of the worst mistakes of all are made in this way (e.g., Revelation for Sunday morning, Daniel for Sunday night, and Ezekiel for Wednesday hardly provide a congregation with a balanced diet!). When you are stuck with a whole book, unwisely selected, you are really stuck! Once chosen, if the choice is bad, it commits a preacher to a long course of error and failure.[2]

However, having wisely chosen a series of studies in a book, then it is easier to bring up difficult or delicate matters *as the book does so,* it is easier to avoid riding one's own personal hobbies, and it saves you the hard work of finding passages on a weekly basis. That in itself can become a frustrating chore.[3]

"Well, then, if I must always begin with a consideration of what will edify the congregation, choosing (at least) the Bible book from which I intend to preach in the light of their needs and circumstances, that requires me to analyze my congregation with accuracy. How do I

2. However, if a preacher errs in making such a selection, and later *recognizes* the fact, he should not persevere in his error out of pride or stubbornness, but simply acknowledge the error to the grateful congregation and make the necessary change *immediately.*

3. Yet, even that problem can be greatly lessened by following the six-month study-and-preparation program that I shall advocate *infra.*

learn to do that?'' That is an important question that must be deferred until a later chapter. For now, we must discuss the matter of the preaching portion in depth.

Let us assume, for simplicity's sake, that you have selected a longer portion from which to preach—a Bible book or a unit of a book large enough that you won't be able to preach on the whole in one sermon. In such a case, the question naturally arises, "How do I divide it into preaching-sized portions?'' Is division an arbitrary matter? Is it determined by the clock on Sunday morning? No. Absolutely not.[4] "Well, then, how do I single out a 'preaching portion,' as you seem to prefer to call it?'' Again, you must make your divisions of the book or unit strictly on the basis of purpose.

Telic Cues

The entire Bible, and any book or portion thereof, may be viewed from the perspective of its *telos* (the New Testament word for "purpose, end, goal, objective"). As a whole, the Bible has a purpose: speaking ultimately, we know that its *telos* is to glorify God.[5] Less ultimately, Jesus said that the Bible's purpose is to help men to love God and their neighbors properly. These purposes, fulfilled, lead to the ultimate one. More proximately speaking, we may mention the purposes (*tele*) detailed in II Timothy 3:15-17; these purposes, fulfilled, cause men to love God and neighbors. These overarching *tele* must be kept in mind at all times when considering the *telos* of any Bible book or lesser portion from it. Every message preached ought to have its relationship to the greater *telos* or *tele* in which the preaching portion is found. This process of discovering, recognizing, and using

4. As a matter of fact, beyond reasonable limits, the clock should be ignored. There is no reason why every sermon should be half an hour or three quarters of an hour long. The preacher should take as long as it requires to preach any given message, whether one week he preaches for 20 minutes or the next for an hour. The passage should determine the sermon length.

5. That idea isn't a pious platitude when properly understood. For a discussion of the biblical concept of doing things to the glory of God, see my book, *Back to the Blackboard* (Phillipsburg, N.J.: Presbyterian and Reformed Publishing Co., 1982), a book that deals with a biblical approach to Christian education.

tele within *tele* continues downward until you select the preaching portion itself:

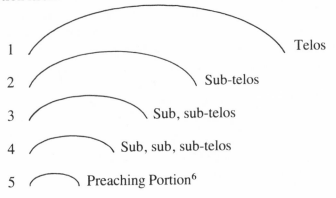

1   Telos

2   Sub-telos

3   Sub, sub-telos

4   Sub, sub, sub-telos

5   Preaching Portion[6]

Each Bible book has its *telos* and its *tele*. For instance, the Gospel of John was written with an overall evangelistic *telos:*

> Now Jesus did many other signs in the disciples' presence that aren't written in this book, but these are written so that you may believe that Jesus is the Christ, God's Son, and that by believing you may have eternal life in His name (John 20:30, 31).

On the other hand, its sequel, I John, was written for an edificational purpose (to bring assurance to converts):

> I have written these things to you who believe in the Name of God's Son that you may know that you have eternal life (I John 5:13).

Jude tells us the *telos* of his book in verse 3. It is interesting to note how Jude discusses purpose. Originally, he tells us, he had an entirely different *telos* in mind when he thought of writing. But news of false teachers and the effect they were having on the church motivated him to change his *telos*.

The *telos* or *tele* of a Bible book is not always spelled out so clearly

---

6. Of course, at any stage, a sermon could have been preached. Stages one to five could each have been considered a preaching portion since each constitutes a telic unit.

by the writer. Often you must discover these for yourself. For instance, John doesn't say in so many words that the *telos* of his second letter is to warn against extending hospitality to false teachers, or that the *telos* of the third letter is to encourage Gaius that he has been right in extending hospitality to true teachers, despite Diotrophes' words and actions, but a study of these two writings makes this clear.

On the other hand, a careful study of Philippians indicates that there were at least four major *tele* behind the writing of that letter:

1. To thank the church for its gift;
2. To ease their concern over Epaphroditus' health;
3. To explain Paul's imprisonment;[7]
4. To deal with the split in the church.

When preaching from Philippians, then, you must keep not only the general purposes of the Bible before you, and the more proximate ones, but the particular one of the four purposes in which your preaching portion is found. That means, for example, that the great christological passage in Philippians 2 ought never be preached in the abstract, totally unrelated to the practical issue of unity of which it forms a part. And even that matter of unity must be oriented to the larger *tele* to which the whole Bible addresses itself (that is to say, unity is not to be urged because it is pleasant, or better for all concerned, but because of its effect on God's church, which in turn has an effect on the honor of His Name).

Determining the Spirit's *telos* of a passage is one of the most important obligations in preaching, perhaps the greatest of all, about which I shall have more to say in the next chapter. But, for now, let me say that a failure to do so constitutes an affront to the Holy Spirit.

Now, let us see how purpose (*telos*) is the determining factor in the selection of the preaching portion. All arbitrary factors in selecting the amount of Scripture from which to preach a given sermon must be abandoned. Blackwood, for instance, used to say, "Preach on a paragraph." While you may often find yourself doing so, that is not what you will always be doing, nor is it a good rule even most of

---

7. For more on this point, see my book, *How to Handle Trouble*.

the time. It is too arbitrary. In the historical books, you may find that you must preach on a chapter—or even two! When preaching in Proverbs, you will often preach on a verse.

What, then, is the determining factor? Purpose. You may preach on *any* purpose unit—regardless of its length. Purpose is what defines a preaching unit. If the Holy Spirit has determined to do something specific by means of *a unit of material devoted to that particular purpose,* then it is clear that it may (must) be preached in order to achieve that very purpose.

Because a purpose, or *telic* unit, determines the preaching unit, it is possible to preach on the *telos* of an entire book or on any sub-*tele;* sub, sub-*tele;* sub, sub, sub-*tele,* etc. So long as a portion of the Scriptures is defined as a unit devoted to producing a particular effect (i.e., achieving a specific purpose), it is proper to preach on it.

Often homileticians have stressed unity as important to a sermon, but, again, they have done so arbitrarily, by fiat. The reason why a sermon ought to treat one major subject, thus creating and preserving unity, is not for literary reasons—balance, symmetry, and the like— but in order to focus on and remain true to the purpose or intention of the Holy Spirit. When you get a hold on some purpose that He had in view, and make that the purpose of your sermon, it is the Holy Spirit's intention that brings unity to the sermon, not some extraneous, arbitrary factor or rhetorical canon.

"But," you may ask, "when you speak of a *telic,* or purpose, unit, just what are you talking about?" The answer to that crucial question will take us into the next chapter.

Class Assignment:

Divide the Book of Jude into preaching portions according to *tele*. Be prepared to show how each portion you have isolated is a *telic* unit. Relate each sub-*telos* to the overall *telos* of the book.

6

DETERMINING
THE *TELOS*

There are few deficiencies in preaching quite so disastrous in their effect as the all-too-frequently occurring failure to determine the *telos* (or purpose) of a preaching portion. The passage, and therefore the Word of God itself, is misrepresented, misused, and mishandled when its purpose has not been determined, with the direct result that its power and its authority are lost. For the preacher we may say, "Get the *telos;* in all your getting, get the purpose." You must never preach on a passage until you are certain you understand why the Holy Spirit included that passage in the Bible. When you have grasped His purpose, what He intended to do to the recipient of His message, then—and then *only*—do you have the purpose for your sermon, and then—and then only—do you know what God wants you to do to your listeners through it. Everything in the sermon—the organization of the material into an outline, the style (language usage), the delivery (use of voice and body)—should contribute to, and therefore be conditioned by, the purpose; everything must further the Holy Spirit's intention in the passage.

When I speak of the purpose or the *telos* of a preaching portion, I refer to the purpose that the Holy Spirit had when He "moved" the writer to pen the words of that passage. That purpose was *broader* than the immediate purpose in the writer's mind when writing to a particular person or church. Paul himself makes this point when he uses Old Testament passages in New Testament contexts:

> Now these events happened as examples for us so that we might not desire evil things as they did (I Cor. 10:6).

> Now these events happened to them as examples and were recorded as counsel for us who live at this late date in history (I Cor. 10:11).

Note also his words in I Corinthians 9:9, 10:

> It is written in Moses' law, "Don't muzzle an ox when it is threshing." It isn't about oxen that God is concerned, is it? Isn't He really speaking about us? It was written for us, because when the plowman plows and the thresher threshes he should do so in hope of having a share of the crop.

Paul himself determined that the *telos* of the Holy Spirit was broader than the situation to which the passage in Deuteronomy 25:4 originally was addressed. He saw that the Holy Spirit's intention in it was *to teach a principle* that was of greater value than when it was originally applied to oxen. The principle, stated in verse 10^b is that the one who works at a task ought to share in its benefits. He clearly applies it to his day, when, in his own words, he writes in verse 14:

> In the same way the Lord gave orders that those who announce the good news should live by announcing the good news (I Cor. 9:14).

So, it must be understood that when I say that the intention of the Holy Spirit must be discovered, I do not mean merely His intention *in its limited application* to an event at the time when the passage was written, but any and all valid applications that He intended to make from any principles that may be generalized from the basic thrust of the passage. The Holy Spirit does not intend for us to use a passage allegorically—finding hidden meanings in every word and generating all sorts of unintended principles from any given passage, but neither does He want us to landlock a principle so that it may be used only when a situation of *exactly* the same sort occurs in our day. No, it is only when a situation arises to which the *telic* principle (i.e., the one, and only the one, that the Holy Spirit had in mind in relationship to His purpose) applies that it is to be used. I shall have more to say on this matter.

The thing to be avoided at all costs is to *impose* your own purposes on the passage. You must be extremely careful not to allow this to happen. Plainly, the history of preaching and sermon analysis shows that this is what has been done again and again. More often than not, if a sermon has a discernible purpose at all, that purpose turns out to be the preacher's purpose rather than the purpose of the Holy Spirit. What you must work for is to make His purpose your own.

To be just to any human writer, his purpose in a given writing must be considered, and purposes that he did not have in mind should not be attributed to him. This book, for instance, should not be used to set forth my views on pastoral counseling; it was not written for that purpose, and it would be misused and I would be misrepresented by anyone who was foolish enough to do such a thing. I have written extensively on counseling; my views on the subject should be gleaned from those books, not from this one. I do not expect someone to treat my writings that way; you would not think of doing that—it would be foolish and would yield strange and perverse results. And yet, that is precisely what preachers do with the writings of the Holy Spirit—not merely human writings—all the time! If you carefully abide by the canon of using a purely human writing for the purposes for which it was intended, how much more careful should you be when using the writings of God? Because you are working in such sacred territory, be careful what you do!

The Holy Spirit, using human authors with the peculiarities of their style and vocabularies (providentially developed, to be sure), preserved them from error in order to set forth the truth that He would use to achieve various purposes He had in mind. That is why it is our duty to become expert exegetes who learn how to determine His purpose in every passage before preaching it.

Historical-grammatical exegesis is essential, but not enough.

Biblical-theological and systematic-theological studies of the passage likewise are important but, again, are insufficient. Rhetorical and literary analyses (areas themselves rarely acknowledged and so usually ignored) are also significant but still do not go far enough. The result of *all* the work done in these six ways will be uselessness, leading at length to frustration and to all sorts of possible harm if you do not go on to discern, *from all those efforts,* the *telos* of the passage. Indeed, all six of these important and essential efforts in studying the passage should be made *telically.* That is to say, there should be purpose in doing what is done. That purpose should be not merely to "understand the passage," if by that you mean to understand what the words mean, but should include the purpose of discovering purpose.

It is only when a preacher knows he is saying what the Holy Spirit said, for the purpose of the Holy Spirit in saying it, that he speaks with power and with authority. This, in part, is what made the difference between Christ and the Pharisees:

> And the result was that when Jesus finished these sayings, the crowds were astonished at His teaching since He taught them as an authority and not as their scribes (Matt. 7:28, 29).

All through the preceding Sermon on the Mount, Jesus corrected the faulty use the scribes (religious teachers) had made of Old Testament Scriptures. That is what He was doing when He said, "You have heard . . . but I say." He was not setting His teaching over against Old Testament teaching; no, exactly not that. He was setting the true *telos* of the Old Testament passages that had been misused by the scribes over against their false interpretations and the wrong purposes for which they used them.

A good example of this is found in Matthew 5:31, 32. The Holy Spirit's purpose in Deuteronomy 24 was not to teach that a bill of divorcement must be given, as the false teachers said. Rather, it was to control and discourage divorce and make clear that divorce on the wrong basis would set up conditions for committing adultery.[1] The

---

1. For more on the specific issues involved, see my book, *Marriage, Divorce and Remarriage in the Bible.*

issue was the intention or purpose of the passage. Christ, unlike the scribes, revealed the *telic* import of Deuteronomy 24; in contrast, they had used the passage for their own ends.

This matter of purpose is such an important consideration in preaching that if your wife were to awaken you on Sunday morning at 4 o'clock and ask, "What is the purpose of this morning's message?" you ought to be able to rattle it off in one crisp sentence, roll over and go to sleep again, all without missing a single stroke in your snoring! Indeed, I think it would be advisable for you to write out at the top of every sermon outline (I'll discuss the other purposes of the outline later) a one-sentence purpose statement. Until you can capsulize the purpose of the sermon in one crisp sentence, you probably do not yet have it clearly enough fixed in your own mind—even if you think you do.

Fundamentally, there are three general purposes in view: to inform, to convince (to believe or disbelieve), or to motivate the members of the congregation in ways that will bring glory to God's Name by building up His church. Here is a typical purpose statement that might appear on the outline: "My purpose is to convince the congregation that Christ is at work in trouble for good." Of course the three general purposes may converge in a message, but when they do, one of the three will be uppermost. The specific purpose is what, specifically, the congregation should learn, believe/disbelieve, or do.

How are you to discover the Holy Spirit's *telos* in a passage of Scripture? Having done your work, you must ask, "Now, what does all this amount to?" More often than not, when you develop a *telic* concern, you will find yourself discovering the *telos* while you are involved in doing the exegesis. All along, at each step during every aspect of the process of preparation, you ought to have some such thought as this in mind: "Now, I wonder just what the Holy Spirit is up to in this passage?" If you do, the *telos* will come clear, usually during, but if not, almost always at the end of, the process of preparation.

Then too, quite frequently you will discover in the passage what I like to call *telic cues*. These are cues to the purpose of a book or a

passage that appear in the passage itself. Once you become aware of
these cues to the purpose of a passage, you will begin to see them
everywhere. Look at the *telic* cue in I Thessalonians 4:13: "Now, we
don't want you to be ignorant, brothers, concerning. . . ." Clearly,
that cue indicates a desire on the part of Paul/the Holy Spirit to *inform*.
But, to provide information is not the sole purpose of the passage. We
know that from the additional *telic* cue appended at the end: ". . . encourage one another with these words." That shows a *motivational*
concern.

Let's consider Luke 15, a passage that has commonly been misused
because those misusing it have failed to recognize and take their cue
from the *telically* oriented words at the outset (vv. 1-3):

> Now the tax collectors and sinners were coming near to listen to
> Him. But the Pharisees and the scribes grumbled, saying, "This
> person welcomes sinners and eats with them." So He told them
> this parable.

You can see that the parables that follow are designed to expose the sin
of those who grumbled over Christ's loving concern to save the
outcasts of society. His purpose in Luke 15, though closely related to
His evangelistic effort, was *not* to do evangelism, as so many have
thought. It had to do rather with hindering the witness to the lost and
the assimilation of new converts into the church. It is wrong to preach
each of these parables separately because, as the context shows, they
all hang together and because, together, they make an impact that can
be made in no other way. Note, a similar pattern runs through each of
the three parables:

1. Something is lost (a sheep, a coin, a son);
2. A search is made;
3. The item is found;
4. Everyone rejoices.

Surely the listeners could do nothing other than *agree* that that is how
it is and, indeed, how it *ought* to be. But just as the Pharisees and the
scribes were nodding assent for the third time, Jesus threw them a
curve. He extended the third parable to reveal the sinful, selfish
attitudes and actions of the elder brother, who, against all reason and

love, was totally out of accord with the appropriate response. This brother, of course, represented the grumblers mentioned in verses 1-3, who had been complaining about the kind of people Jesus was associating with. They complained, "This person welcomes sinners and eats with them" (v. 2).

The power and intent of the passage is lost when the parables are pried apart and, apart from their intended purpose, are used for evangelistic purposes. Surely, the gospel is in them as Christ "seeks and saves that which is lost," but that isn't the prime thrust. Convicting those snobbish and self-righteous parishioners who have problems in welcoming previously notorious and unkempt converts into the church would provide a much more appropriate use of the passage that lines up with its *telic* principle.

It is possible, of course, to preach on sub-*tele so long as* (1) there are sub-*tele* in the passage (there do not seem to be any in Luke 15), (2) you do so in a way that recognizes the larger *telic* thrust of which it is a sub-category, and (3) you do not distort the *telos* or *tele* of which the sub-*telos* is a purpose unit. In using it you must show how it relates to and contributes to the *telos* or *tele* of which it is a part. It is possible to spend the major portion of a sermon informing the congregation about the coming of Christ and the resurrection of the dead who go out to escort Him as He returns, but it would be altogether wrong to lose sight of the purpose of such explanations—to comfort and encourage grief-stricken and confused believers.

For more on *telos* in preaching, see my two articles on the subject in a book of essays on preaching, *Truth Apparent,* as well as the discussion on the subject in *What to Do on Thursday,* a book on the practical use of the Scriptures, and *Lectures on Counseling,* pages 198-203. All these books are published by the Presbyterian and Reformed Publishing Company, Phillipsburg, New Jersey 08865.

Class Assignments:

1. Read and report on the materials on *telos* in one of the three books mentioned above.
2. Find the *telos* of five passages of Scripture and write them out in a telic statement.

7

ANALYZING
THE CONGREGATION

We have already seen in chapter 5 that the prime purpose in analyzing a congregation is to select just those passages and books that will come closest to meeting the needs of the congregation. These will vary from congregation to congregation because of dissimilar backgrounds and unique current problems, opportunities, and influences. So, it is essential for a Bible-believing pastor to know how to analyze and adapt his preaching to each congregation in particular.[1]

There are three principal ways in which a faithful pastoral preacher may analyze his congregation:

1. by means of informal contacts;
2. by means of counseling contacts;
3. by means of formal contacts.

All three should be used since they tend to supplement one another.

---

1. For information on how Paul adapted his preaching to different audiences—even in one-encounter evangelistic contexts—see my book, *Audience Adaptation in the Sermons and Speeches of Paul*.

Informal Contacts

The informal contact is the fundamental and basic source of information from which congregational analyses may be made. Contacts of this sort are made while rubbing shoulders with members of the congregation as, together, you are involved in church work, but also, and indeed especially, as you do things together in even more informal contexts. The preacher who remains in his study day and night, and who emerges only to attend some formal function of the body, may think that he knows his people, but, as far as knowing their needs, he is really out of touch with them. It is one thing to speak to people at board meetings, in prayer meetings, and after church services; it is quite another to chat during a ball game, at a picnic, or when painting a building. A different side of the individual shows in these two kinds of contexts. Moreover, it is one thing to observe a member in action on church turf but quite another to watch him in his home, in his office, or at a school board hearing. To put it simply, in order to preach to people as they really are, you must see and hear them as they really are. So much of what they do and say while on the church premises is what they think is expected of them; how they are elsewhere often may more nearly approximate their actual inward state.

Time spent informally with the members of one's congregation, then, is not wasted time. Hours of conversation, of work or pleasure spent together with members of the congregation, for the man who rightly uses them, can be among the most valuable ones in the week when it comes to gathering the materials that are necessary to make good choices for future sermons. However, the preacher must be careful to get around to large numbers of his members (all, in time) and not confine his contacts to a small group of persons. Otherwise, he will distort the general picture by limiting his sample to an unrepresentative minority. If there is no other way, he can at least invite various persons to his home for a treat following the Sunday evening service. Of course, these contacts should not be made merely to gather information for congregational analysis; the pastor should genuinely try to get to know each person as a friend. The material for analysis will arise naturally; he will not need to "pump" people. Such material comes best when not sought, but when the preacher is alert and always ready to receive what is freely offered.

It is easy to get a distorted view of the congregation by limiting one's contacts. This readily happens because there are people with whom you will find that it is much easier to make friendships, while there are others with whom that is a very difficult thing to do. You will enjoy spending time with some; it will be hard to spend time with others. But a faithful minister of the Word himself will be a friend of all. He will be aware of the temptations and difficulties, guard against failure, and make every legitimate effort to break through barriers.

Counseling

People come to pastors with problems. When you discover an inordinate number of instances in which the same or a similar problem occurs, you should investigate the matter thoroughly to discover the reason. Perhaps there has been erroneous, insufficient, or inadequate teaching in the past; perhaps there is a lack of church care and discipline at this point; possibly there are perverse influences at work among the members of the body.

Moreover, as you counsel members, patterns will emerge. Not only will you discover the original areas in which problems are commonly arising, but you will also notice the futile, sinful, unbiblical ways in which your people attempt to solve these problems, ways that, instead, serve only to complicate, deepen, and extend them. And you will begin to note the unbiblical sources to which they have been turning for help and what pernicious damage has been done by following them. All this—and much more—will emerge in counseling and will provide insight in determining what you ought to be preaching about.

The preacher who does not counsel makes a grave mistake. Not only does he fail to fulfil his dual commission to be a *pastor*-teacher, but his teaching also will be adversely affected. Paul elsewhere fused the two-pronged ministry of the Word together when he spoke of teaching "publicly and from house to house" (Acts 20:20). The public proclamation of the Word was accompanied by its private application to individuals and families in counseling. Paul also quite firmly linked the two in Colossians 1:28 when he wrote:

> Whom we announce, counseling every person and teaching every person as wisely as possible, so that we may present every person mature in Christ.

To "present every person mature in Christ" requires both public preaching and private counseling.

But it is not the mere fact of the unity of the one ministry of the Word in both its more general and its more specific aspects that I wish to note. In addition, I want you to see that, being a unity, the two manifestations of this ministry cannot be split apart without injury to each; they function properly when they function in tandem.

Counseling requires preaching just as preaching requires counseling. One reason why counselors who do not preach fail to become as biblical as they might is that they are not required to do exegesis on a regular basis. That means they can limp along (that is to say, they *think* they can) with whatever biblical knowledge they have or may glean from weekly church attendance. Time that a pastor would devote to the biblical exegesis counselors often spend studying counseling literature and for lack of biblical understanding, adopt into their practice ideas that conflict with God's truth. Because of life's pressures, because of the laziness of sinful human beings, and because of the many temptations to do otherwise, most counselors need the enforced discipline of having to prepare sermons each week to keep them studying the Bible regularly in an intensive way.

The counselor who preaches each week will grow as a counselor. He will gain new biblical insights from his weekly study that he will incorporate into counseling, and he will develop the assurance and sure-footedness that is necessary to counsel with biblical authority. Many counselors who do not have a growing biblical underpinning to their counseling naturally adopt a non-judgmental, non-directive approach. If they tried to be directive, they would hardly know what to say with any true assurance.

But the pastoral preacher also benefits from counseling; and that is our present concern. If he is not truly a *pastoral* preacher—i.e., one who meets the needs of the flock, giving individual attention to the sheep—he will not preach well. If he spends his time during the week with commentaries alone, when he preaches he will sound like a book. But the man who puts his exegesis to work, not just on Sunday in the pulpit, but all week long in the counseling room, ministering the Word to those in trouble, will rattle his people's windows when he preaches. They will say to themselves, "He understands!" And they will come for help. Each activity feeds the other.

Moreover, the counseling preacher can work preventively. What he regularly sees in the study he can warn against in the pulpit. What he learns about people, and his people in particular, he can use (properly, of course—no confidences will be disclosed) to the advantage of all. Nothing enables a preacher to ring the bell in a Sunday sermon like knowing that in counseling he has already helped five persons with what he is about to say. It is questionable whether you are ever ready to preach from a passage until you have already used the passage (or one with the same *telos*) successfully in your own life and in counseling others. Passages preached after successful use elsewhere are preached differently from those preached *de novo*.[2] You will find that such use puts a patina on your preaching of truth that can come only from loving wear and tear.

Formal Analysis

In a sense, you are always analyzing congregational members if you love them and care for their welfare. You develop a sensitivity to congregational needs akin to the sensitivity that a mother has for her baby's needs. That, of course, is in accord with the idea that leaders

2. This is only another reason for the six-month study-preparation program that I shall present in chapter 13.

are to "keep watch" over the flock (cf. Heb. 13:17).[3] At all times you will be alert to the attack of the wolves that stalk the church, to the spiritual diseases that spread among the sheep, to the whereabouts of sheep that are prone to wander, and to all of the many other untoward situations into which a flock can come. From these normal functions of pastoral care, a growing understanding of the congregation's welfare will develop. But these informal analyses, as valuable as they can be, must be supplemented by regular, formal check-ups to discover the state of things.

How can stated, formal analyses of a congregation's growth, or lack of it, best be made?

First of all, let me suggest that on your arrival at a new pastorate, as soon as all your books are on the study shelf, you should make an initial analysis, especially of the preaching that has been done in the recent past. Look for a record of what has been preached over the last three years. Sometimes the church bulletins are bound and kept in the church library. A study of these will tell you a lot (about the preaching and much more).[4] No such book? Then inquire around. You will find a little old lady somewhere who has collected bulletins going back to the First World War. Borrow the recent copies in her collection and survey the menus from which the congregation has been eating. Former pulpit chefs, you may discover, have placed an over-emphasis on sermon salads to the neglect of preaching proteins —or it may be the other way around. You may want to schedule your early preaching to balance out the starchy diet on which your congregation has been subsisting, and you may want to begin to look around among the members for any cases of spiritual rickets that may have resulted from this poorly balanced meal.

Moreover, periodic checks on the state of things at six-month intervals, at the time of your semi-annual planning and preparation effort (I'll discuss this later), will provide just the sort of information you will need to select the books and passages that will fit your congregation most snugly.

3. See also I Thess. 2:7, 8, 11.
4. Be sure you leave one.

"But how do I go about making a formal check or analysis of the congregation?" Of course, there are many sorts of steps you could follow. I shall suggest but a few. First, review your counseling notes for the past six months. See any patterns? Trends? Are you reminded of any needs? Next, visit with a representative group of persons: a couple of teenagers, a young married couple or two, one or two older singles, some retired persons, businessmen, housewives. Find out how they see the situation from where they sit. Put together all the information you have gathered and then evaluate it. Again, any trends? Any deep concerns? What does the information tell you? Thirdly, call a "state of the union" meeting of the elders and discuss the question with them. Probe them deeply. It is their task to *know* what is going on (Heb. 13:17); assume that they do, let them know that you will hold such a meeting every six months, and you probably will begin to notice a growing incisiveness in their responses. They should have much information to contribute. Finally, go over each name on the roll prayerfully and thoughtfully. Try to evaluate each person's situation as best you can. What does he need most from you during the next six months? What are his *immediate* requirements? Answer as fully as you can. Failure to be able to do so will point up to you how much (little) you know about your congregation and especially about particular members of it. This should also lead to plans for deeper contacts whenever these are necessary.

Put down in writing everything you have found. You will have more than you can handle during the next six months if your work has been thorough. So you'll want to begin with this list when you come to your next six months' evaluation. Also, review of the list at that time will enable you to check up on any progress or the lack of it, and the list, during the next six months, will provide a prayer guide for you. You will probably want to plan for a few days of isolation every six months to work on these matters.

What are you looking for when you make such analyses? What you want to find are the areas in which you can build up the church. These will include neglected areas, areas in which failure is occurring, etc. If, according to the construction analogy lying behind the word "edify," you look at the church as an uncompleted building, a building on which at times inferior workmanship has been done, and a building that from time to time has been vandalized while under construction, in most cases you will not be far from the right track. You are a builder, supervisor, construction worker, and guard, all rolled into one. You must do, or subcontract to others to whom you delegate the work, what needs to be done. Much of the construction work that lies ahead will have to be done through your preaching and your follow-up on it.

There is one other matter worth mentioning here. You may ask, "Does a pastor decide to preach about a subject, or in an area of concern, simply because it constitutes a majority problem?" What I have said thus far might lead you to believe that I think so. However, there are other considerations. One of the chief of these is the greatness of the danger of a *potential* problem. If some threat to the congregation looms large on the horizon, the preacher may elect to preach about the matter regardless of how few persons (if any) have actually been affected by it. False ideas abroad in the community, whether they be heretical teachings, secularizing and humanistic movements, or the corrupting influences of the media, may trigger sermons launched from their pad like protective, preventive satellites.

It is true, then, to say that whatever builds up the church, and whatever will preserve what has already been built, is what the pastoral preacher looks for.

Class Assignment:

Analyze a congregation in depth with the permission and help of its pastor. Hand in your results in a major paper and provide a copy for the pastor.

THE PREACHER'S STANCE

I write you a letter asking you to help me to obtain the position of associate pastor in your church. You read the letter closely, noting exactly what each word and phrase means. You find out all about me and the circumstances under which the letter was written. Then, after all this effort, and much more like it with which I shall not bore you, you say, "Well, I've finally got it. I understand what this letter is all about: Adams wants to be my associate pastor." And that's it; that's where it all ends!

Strange? Of course. Absurd? Naturally. We don't ordinarily do things like that. I expect a certain kind of response to my request, and you, surely, would give me one. The purpose of the letter was to elicit a yes or no response, which would lead to further action on my part and might also lead to further action from you and from the church. The letter could cause a number of changes.

We are continually concerned about the lack of change that preaching brings about. One of the reasons there is no more response is the stance the speaker takes toward the Bible and his congregation, and the stance he urges them to take toward the Bible. When his stance is wrong, he can expect theirs to be wrong too. No wonder so little change takes place; much so-called "preaching" does not require it.

Much "preaching" is every bit as inappropriate as your hypothetical response to the letter mentioned above. The preacher does a good job of considering the historical-grammatical exegesis of the preaching passage, considers it theologically and rhetorically, and then—simply tells his congregation what it means. His response, and consequently theirs as well, is to say, "Well, now I understand it," and that's that! That is not preaching. True preaching does all of the above, but it also identifies the *telos* (purpose) of the passage, builds the message around it, and *calls on the congregation for a response that is appropriate to it*. It works for change.

Preaching that stops short of asking for change that is appropriate to the Holy Spirit's letters to His church is not preaching at all; at best, it is lecturing.

The lecturer speaks *about* the Bible; the pastoral preacher speaks *from* the Bible *about* the congregation. He tells them what God wants from them. These are two distinct stances. Let me see if I can set these two distinct stances over against one another so that the contrast between them will be even more apparent. I shall first set them out in diagram and chart form; then I shall discuss them with you.

LECTURE STANCE   PREACHING STANCE

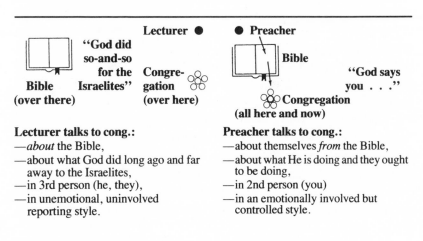

Lecturer talks to cong.:
—*about* the Bible,
—about what God did long ago and far away to the Israelites,
—in 3rd person (he, they),
—in unemotional, uninvolved reporting style.

Preacher talks to cong.:
—about themselves *from* the Bible,
—about what He is doing and they ought to be doing,
—in 2nd person (you)
—in an emotionally involved but controlled style.

Everything that the lecturer says may be quite true, but if that truth doesn't come to grips with the congregation in such a way that it can change their lives in accordance with the purpose of the Holy Spirit, it may be lecturing, but it isn't preaching.

What makes the difference between lecturing and preaching? Stance, as I have said. Well, then, how do the two stances essentially differ?

First, the preacher searches for and discovers the *telos* in his preaching portion and makes the Spirit's purpose his own. The lecturer need not ever discover the *telos*, but if he does, he will not make it his own. It is enough for him to point out that this is what the Spirit had in mind (for the Israelites, David, Paul). The Holy Spirit's purpose in I Thessalonians 4 may be to encourage grief-stricken, confused Christians whose relatives have recently died by presenting facts concerning the coming of Christ, but the lecturer's purpose is simply to recount those facts to his listeners. If he goes so far as to indicate that the Holy Spirit wished to encourage and comfort the Thessalonians, he will go further than many, but he will still not *preach* those facts *in an encouraging way* that is designed to *comfort*. That is because his purpose is not to comfort but to relate facts. The lecturer has but one purpose: to inform. Rarely, if ever, do the Scriptures *merely* inform. As we have seen, information about the Lord's coming is given a motivational twist: "Encourage one another with these words." When they are used to encourage as well as to inform, that is preaching; when they are used simply to inform, that is lecturing. Too much lecturing passes for preaching.

Look at the diagram and the chart. In the typical lecture stance, the lecturer and the congregation stand over against the Bible, in an "objective," uninvolved way. Their stance is *apart from* as well as *over against*. The Bible has become an object of interest and analysis. Their concerns are about what happened in Bible times, not about what happens today. They take the historical viewpoint. Consequently, the language that they use abounds in "he," "she," and "they" constructions. And the past tense predominates.

On the other hand, the pastoral preacher, the congregation, and the

Bible are all bound together in a here-and-now fashion. All three are wrapped up in something that is taking place at the moment, or ought to take place in the near future. There is involvement in the facts. Because the preacher's concern is not to communicate facts but to produce change by facts, he will speak largely in the present tense to the congregation, about God and themselves *on the basis of what God said and did* to others and to them *in Bible times*.

The true preacher will be no less concerned about what happened to Israel and to the Amalekites than is the lecturer. Nor will he take any less care in exegeting the passage and in explaining it to his congregation. But he will do so, from start to finish, with the understanding that this pertains to them, not just to Israel and the Amalekites. The lecturer speaks about the Bible, and about David; so does the preacher. But the preacher does so to demonstrate to the congregation that this is the basis and authority he has for what he is saying about God and *them*. And, whereas the "scholarly" lecturer stands aloof from the data as a reporter of facts, never allowing the data to touch him, the pastoral preacher is willing to enter into the full weight of its emotional impact for himself and for his people. Preaching engages the whole person, not the intellect only.

The lecturer is concerned about literary analysis; that is why he thinks in terms of the "central idea" or "theme" of a passage rather than about its *telos*. The preacher is concerned about people; that is why he is oriented toward what the Holy Spirit intends to do for them through preaching that passage. It is for that reason that preachers today, like those in the Book of Acts, so frequently use the second person.

Until your stance toward the Bible, God, and your congregation is proper, you will never really preach as you should. This is a vital issue. Try as you may, you will find it as impossible to do so as if you were to take a pitcher's stance while up at bat. It is all a matter of stance. Stance has to do with how you orient and address yourself toward something or someone. The purpose of learning to develop a correct stance, then, is to enable one to do well what he wishes to do. Some would-be preachers have been more concerned about their golf stance and how they address the ball than about their preaching stance and how they address their people.

So, if stance is all-important, as indeed it is, then be sure that your stance is a preaching stance and not a lecturing stance. To preach with ease and with power in a manner that fully honors the Spirit and His Word requires it.

Class Assignment:

Analyze three printed sermons for their stance. Be prepared to report on and discuss *one*.

9

A PREACHING OUTLINE

"Why are you considering outlining before you focus on content?" Because we are preachers of the Word, not rhetoricians. Our basic content comes from the Bible and not from other sources.[1] Of course, it might be appropriate to discuss exegesis and hermeneutics for several chapters, but that is beyond the purpose and scope of this book. I must assume (and I know this is a very large assumption) you know how to exegete according to proper hermeneutical methods.

Having assumed that and, further, having assumed you have successfully completed the study of a passage, let us consider what you will do with your findings. First, let us ask, what do you have at this point? Perhaps, following your exegetical study, you now have in your possession something like the following:

1. Notes on the meaning of the passage, with cross references, word studies, etc. You may have made your own translation of it. All this is recorded on several sheets of paper, note cards, or in a notebook.

---

1. I shall speak of illustrative materials, etc., at a later point.

47

2. Jottings of various sorts, including
   a. ideas suggested by the exegetical study;
   b. initial outlines, or bits of outlines, that occurred to you during the study;
   c. illustrations;
   d. possibly a suggested title or two.
3. A crisp, one-sentence *telic* statement.
4. Initial ideas about how to introduce and/or close the sermon.
5. Extraneous materials (not always seen as such at first) that will best be laid aside and filed for future use.
6. A list of problems and questions yet unresolved and unanswered.

It is at this point that organizing your materials into an outline becomes a vital matter. "Organizing, yes," you say, "but what is the purpose of the outline?" Its main purpose is to cue the preacher. But this cuing is not merely a matter of jogging foggy memories; more than that—it must be his cue to *preach* rather than to *lecture*.

Some preachers write and read, or write, memorize, and recite rather than speak. You should be clear about one thing: reading and reciting are not speaking. There is no evidence whatever in the Bible that anyone ever wrote out and read, or memorized and recited, a sermon or talk. But there is plenty of genuine speaking! Speaking differs from reading and reciting in many ways; people in general cannot tell you precisely what these differences are, but in most cases they surely can tell the difference. Written and oral English are quite distinct (I have compared and contrasted the two in depth in *Pulpit Speech*).[2] The highest praise a reader can receive is, "I didn't even know you were reading; you sounded so natural." Why not be "natural," then? Why not give people what they expect from a speaker rather than an imitation of the real thing, no matter how successful that imitation may be? Surely it is not too much to ask of a minister that he learn how to stand up and speak!

Extemporaneous speaking does not necessarily mean unprepared, impromptu speaking. Good preaching is thoroughly prepared in form as well as content. The organization and order are planned, as well as

2. Pp. 113ff.

the content. What are not planned are most of the words, phrases, and sentences the preacher will use. These will be chosen by him on the spot. Exact sentences, except perhaps for a few especially in the introduction and conclusion, will not be prepared beforehand. Words will be snapped together to form sentences as the preacher moves along. That should not be such a formidable task; we are all accustomed to speaking extempore with far less preparation all the time. Why, then, shouldn't a minister be able to think and speak on his feet, especially when he has the substance of what he wants to say on an outline to which he may refer at any time he wishes?

The method of using a full outline allows for the best of both worlds. It provides for the security, order, and precision of written sermons while at the same time allowing freedom to adapt to circumstances and to benefit from the "jelling factor."[3] All in all, the full sentence outline, therefore, seems to be the best way to go.

What do I mean by a "full sentence outline"? Just that: an outline composed of complete sentences. So often we think that we understand something when we don't, if we write only a word or a phrase. Moreover, you may understand now, and the single word or phrase may serve you well to trigger your memory now, but five years from now, in another pastorate and hundreds of sermons (with words and phrases) later—will it still do so? Probably not. The full sentence outline, however, will preserve your thought. That is another purpose for it.

Now, I suggest also that you print out the sermon by hand; doing so gives you flexibility. For instance, major points can be made to stand out by enlarging them; at a glance, with a glance, you can read them in the pulpit without searching. Other points, probably not needed in the pulpit, but there for future preservation, and there in the pulpit *just in case,* may be lettered by hand in smaller print. Here is how a slice of the body of such a sermon outline might look:

---

3. See information later on about this matter.

> I. GOD FORBIDS YOU TO WORRY
>   A. He says "Don't worry"
>   B. About "anything"
>   1. That means your checkbook
>   2. That means your family
>
>   C. To do so is sin
>   D. cf. Mt. 6:34
> II. GOD COMMANDS YOU TO PRAY
>   A. In everything
>   B. With thanksgiving
>   1. Even for the cut in salary
>   2. About the difficulty with Bill

As you can see, at a single glance you can pick up each major point. These major points I always underline with a felt tip pen in green; Bible references are underlined in red, and illustrative material in blue. If I need to refer to this material—I often take a look at Bible references (to be sure) before announcing them, and sometimes I want to use some exact wording in illustrative material—again at a glance, I can instantly spot any information I need while I am preaching. Some such method may prove useful to you too.

Now, because this is a homiletic textbook and not a book on speech and rhetoric, in it I should not have to show you how to organize and outline material in terms of coordinate and subordinate points, etc. Yet I know from experience in teaching that many seminary students—

and even some pastors—are very deficient in these matters. Yet, I cannot bring myself to clutter these pages with such things. (If you need help—and you should be honest about the matter—consult my more basic book, *Pulpit Speech*.[4]) Instead, I want to talk about a matter that can't be found in speech books or, for that matter, in homiletic textbooks either: it is the importance of developing a *preaching* outline.

"What makes an outline a *preaching* outline?" you may wonder. That is what I want you to consider. If the basic purpose of an outline is to cue the preacher, then the outline should cue him to *preach*. Many men who want to preach, rather than to lecture, find themselves hindered by wrong signals emanating from their outlines, which cue them wrongly.

Just as many (perhaps most) preachers lecture rather than preach, and they are concerned about central ideas, themes, and the like, rather than about purpose, so too do they develop outlines that are suited not to preaching but to lecturing. They don't know any better—that is how they were taught—and as a result find themselves cued by the outline for lecturing, which they then proceed to do—on cue. Even if they wanted to preach according to those outlines, they would find themselves frustrated at every point. When they abandon the lecture platform and turn to preaching, they will have to dispose of their former outlines as surely as the Ephesians burned their magic books.

The lecture format and the preaching format, just like the lecture stance and the preaching stance, contrast with one another in every vital respect:

Lecture Format	*Preaching Format*
1. Then and there	1. Here and now
2. Third person emphasis	2. Second person emphasis
3. Abstract	3. Concrete
4. In terms of others	4. In terms of the congregation
5. Informative	5. Persuasive or motivational

4. If this textbook is used in a formal course, it would be well to have a few copies of *Pulpit Speech* on reserve, and to give some assignments from it as need arises.

At the top of a lecture outline, under the title, will be a thematic statement or statement of the central idea:

"The theme of this sermon [*sic*] is daily prayer."

In a true preaching outline there will be, at the top of the outline, not a thematic statement, but a *telic* (or purpose) statement that will look something like this:

"My purpose is to encourage you to pray daily."

Compare and contrast the two; can't you see the difference already? Notice how the thematic statement orients and cues the speaker to *lecture about a topic* as *information*, while the purpose statement prepares him to *preach to people* about their *lives?*

But the contrast does not stop with the cuing statement at the top of the outline. It extends to the entire outline. Here, again, are two examples:

Lecture Format	*Preaching Format*
The Gifts of the Spirit	Use Your Spiritual Gifts
I. The source of the Corinthians' gift.	I. God gave each of you gifts.
II. The function of the Corinthians gift.	II. God gave you them to use.
III. The purpose of the Corinthians' gift.	III. God gave them to use for the benefit of others.

Notice the differences, not only in the titles, but throughout. Of course, I have included only the major heads, but the same thing holds true for subordinate points that is true for these major heads.

1. These titles differ:
   —One is abstract, the other personal.
   —One is factual, the other is motivational.
2. The main points are different:
   —Those in one are abstract, in the other personal.
   —In one, the focus is on the Corinthians, in the other on the congregation.

You can see clearly, can't you, that the preaching format continually cues the preacher to be personal, to address his congregation, to bring them face to face with God and His requirements; in short, it cues him to preach. The lecture format cues the speaker to lecture *about,* not to preach *to.*

Notice the abstract terms "source, function, purpose" in the first outline. Words like these put congregations to sleep. They do not say anything helpful. They are abstract and analytical and squeeze all the juice out of a text and its truth. Actually, they could be used in any talk. Indeed, the way some preachers use such terms, they might as well mimeograph two or three such "universal outlines" with blanks to fill in.

   I. The Source of _____

  II. The Function of _____

 III. The Purpose of _____

or

   I. The Nature of _____

  II. The Purpose of _____

 III. The Results of _____

These are not preaching outlines; they are outlines of analytical studies of a topic. It is possible for you to speak for 40 to 45 minutes from a lecture outline of this sort and yet never tell the congregation anything about themselves and what God expects of them.

One way in which the preaching outline, cast in its preaching format, helps the preacher to accomplish his purpose is by forcing him—if he follows it—to apply the truth of his passage to the congregation throughout. Notice how each point is made *to the congregation.* A preaching outline is the outline of a *message,* an outline of a talk directed to people in order to change them in some way that God wants to see them changed. A lecture outline is the outline of a talk, designed to inform, but not necessarily to change. It is *not* a message; it is a learned discourse on a subject. It hangs facts out on the line to flap in the breeze. A preaching outline is designed to thrust truth into the midst of lives in order to change those lives.

When preachers who use the lecture format (inherited from the medieval scholastics through the English Puritans) realize that they must apply the passage, what they usually do is to tack on an application at the end. I say "tack on," because it does not naturally fit the lecture format. Here is how it goes: "And now what does all this have to do with us." (Usually a lecturer is deathly afraid of saying "you.") It is a little late, however, to ask that question and to apply something or other that has been discussed for 30-odd minutes in the abstract. The preacher, on the other hand, using a genuine preaching outline, applies all along the way; indeed, in one sense the whole sermon is application. The preaching format is an applicatory format by nature; nothing needs to be "tacked on" (I'll say a lot more about application in a later chapter).

"But doesn't the lecturer say more about the text than does the applicatory preacher?" No. The preacher explains the text just as fully as does the lecturer; in fact, more fully. He explains the *telos* as well. Everything of importance that the lecturer might say about the passage (and, lecturing lends itself to by-paths, discussing *un*important details, it must be remembered) the preacher can say also. The difference is in *how they handle* the same material; the difference is in their orientation and use of it, and in how they say what they say. The lecturer says, "Let us look at the source of the Corinthians' gifts." The preacher says, "This passage teaches that God gave you gifts through the Holy Spirit. See, here it is. . . ." Then he too considers the passage. But the congregation knows *why* they are looking at it when he does. They know that they are discovering what God did for the Corinthians *in order to discover what He does for them*.[5]

Few more important facts could be said about outlining. I have put

5. Of course, there will not always be a one-to-one correspondence. As in this instance, the preacher will be careful to distinguish between the ordinary gifts that are for all and the extraordinary gifts that were given to authenticate the apostles (II Cor. 12:12).

the emphasis where it belongs: be sure your outline is truly a preaching outline.

Here I could have spoken about introductions and conclusions, but I shall reserve that for later. But one word about conclusions in relationship to *telic* statements now, and one other matter, and I shall close this chapter.

One way to check your sermon outline when you have finished sketching it in rough form is to read the purpose statement at the top, which tells you where you intend to go, then read over the conclusion to see if you got there. If, in your *telic* statement, you say, "My purpose is to travel to New York," and in the conclusion you find yourself talking about Washington, D.C., and how you "finally arrived there after a long, hard trip," you know that somewhere in the body of the sermon you took a wrong turn. Go back and look for it. You will find that you did—every time! I know of no more valuable check that you can make to determine the unity and direct line of thought from start to finish. Check out a half dozen of your sermons this way, and you may be surprised to find that you frequently get lost along the way. If you can't steer a straight course, how do you expect your listeners to do so?

The final matter I mentioned is whether or not you should announce main points in your outline to the congregation. Some scholastics insist on it. Should you? Yes and no. As a matter of form, the answer is no; you should have a good purpose for everything you do. It is *not* a good purpose to announce points simply because some scholastic homileticians say so! No, the rule is do nothing unless it serves a useful biblical purpose. You will not want to announce points ordinarily; they will break the flow of the discourse if there is no good reason for announcing them. You will want to announce points *when the fact of "so many points"* or of *"these particular steps"* is of significance to the argument, helps to clarify a concept for the congregation, or enables them to remember something—i.e., when there is a good purpose for doing so. Thus, you may hear yourself from time to time rightly saying, "Now, I want you to know that God requires *two* things of you in this situation, not *one*. He says not only that you must 'put off' your old sinful patterns, but also you must 'put on' new righteous ones. You cannot break habits; you must *replace* them with biblical alternatives. So, remember *two* things are necessary: putting off and putting on. We shall consider each. First, you must put off your old sinful ways. . . ." Here, you can see a good reason for announcing your heads. So many people fail to change because they try to "break" habits, as the world says, considering the process to be single factored. Because you want to *make a point* of the fact that there are *two* steps in the process, you will ring in the changes on those two points throughout. But in a sermon in which there is no point to announcing heads, don't. Whatever serves no good purpose, serves to hinder rather than help. If announcing points does not make a point, don't announce them.

So, in conclusion, much more could be said about outlining and has been said elsewhere. Here, all I wish to say is to be sure that your outline is cast in a preaching format—that is the crucial issue. Why? Because the *purpose* of an outline is to help you to do what you must do: preach!

NOTE

There is one common practice that deserves mention. Often, preachers, especially those who try to "stay close to the text" and so-called "expository" preachers will tell you that they use the structure of the passage to determine the structure of their sermon. Typically you will hear them say things like, "Now this text naturally falls into three divisions." So, it falls into three divisions; so what? Does that mean that sermons from Revelation will have seven points? Will a message from Proverbs always have two because proverbs "naturally" fall into two divisions? Will all preaching from John, with his many contrasts (light/darkness, truth/error, etc.), also be two-pointed? To say that a passage falls into so many divisions may be good literary and rhetorical analysis, but what has that got to do with preaching forms?

What is the purpose of following the "natural textual divisions"?

To be more biblical? To do so doesn't make you more biblical but *less* biblical. Nowhere do you find a biblical preacher saying, "Now my text naturally falls . . ." or anything like it.

Why does a proverb "fall into two divisions"? Not for preaching purposes, but, as I mentioned, because it is a Hebrew poetical form consisting of antithesis or repetition. What you are doing when you allow the form of the text to dictate the form of the sermon, in most cases, makes no sense. You are to preach, *not* to recite poetry; why, then, use a poetical form? The proverbial form is just right for a proverb, but usually it isn't right for preaching. There are narrative, apocalyptic, parabolic, epistolary forms, etc. Each has its own structure, *suited for its own purpose;* but *that purpose isn't preaching.*

Only in some places does another form overlap the preaching form. One reason why Paul's letters, for instance, often nicely accommodate themselves to preaching is that Paul himself was a preacher. When he wrote, he employed an amanuensis, and his dictation often represents the same sort of material he must have taught when he preached in the churches in similar form. Therefore, portions of his letters are in preaching form; indeed, one can even hear Paul's dictation turn into preaching at times as he reads. (For a good study of Paul's edificational preaching, examine his letters.)

But, for the most part, the form in which a passage appears must be "translated" from a narrative form (you are not telling a story), a poetic form (you are not reciting poetry), etc., into a preaching form. Unlike an acrostic poem, designed for memorization, you are preaching, an activity that is designed for change. The design changes the form. A sermon develops its peculiar form from the fact that it is a message to people about their relationship to God. Whatever legitimate ways that best reach people, therefore, are viable in sermon construction; the Bible gives us no set directions about form. But in its own practice the Bible does demonstrate the principle of the use of forms appropriate to one's purpose.

Ordinarily the major thrust of a sermon should come early. Then it may be reinforced by helpful (not unnecessary) repetition, phrased in varied ways, throughout the course of the sermon. But at times, when a congregation is likely to be opposed to a truth, it might be wiser to save the punch line for closer to the end (as Nathan did when addressing David and as Stephen did when preaching to the Jews) in order to get a hearing.

A wide variety of preaching forms is possible, as even a study of New Testament evangelistic preaching reveals. But, unless the passage itself "naturally falls into *preaching* divisions," there is no more warrant for using its structure to govern the sermon structure than to use any other.

Class Assignments:

1. Take an outline of one of your sermons, already written, and test it for its format: Is it cast in a preaching or lecture format? If the former, congratulations! Note its features. If not, "translate" it into a preaching format, personalizing it, updating it to the here and now, etc. Turn in a copy of both.
2. In class, take two or three printed "sermon" outlines that are cast in lecture form. Together, as a class, work on them to recast them in preaching form, using the overhead projector.

10

PURPOSEFUL
INTRODUCTIONS

The purpose of an introduction is to lead the congregation into the matter to be discussed. If it fails to do that, it fails. The preacher has been studying the passage of Scripture from which he will preach, and thinking about it, for some time (in most cases all week long; in my program, *infra,* for six months); presumably, even in the midst of a series of sermons on a Bible book, the congregation has not. They come to the passage cold; that is why an introduction is in order.

A good introduction orients the congregation to what will be said by arresting and interesting the congregation. When you begin to preach, many (perhaps most) of the members of the assembly are thinking of other things.[1] As far as the thrust of your preaching portion is concerned, they will be disoriented. So you must orient them to it by what you say at the beginning.

Orienting a congregation, as I said, involves arresting attention and creating interest. Arresting, or getting attention, is absolutely essen-

1. A properly designed and effected worship service will do much to keep minds from wandering, to create a state of expectancy, and to prepare the way for the message, even as the message complements, and often climaxes, what has come before.

tial; until you have done so, the congregation will hear nothing that you have to say, no matter how valuable or interesting it may be. But, on the other hand, once you have gained a hearing you must hold it. That is done by creating interest. It is of little value to gain attention if that is not immediately turned into interest. The function of a good introduction is to do both. How, then, may you orient a congregation to God's message by arresting and holding their attention?

The first factor is to begin with the congregation itself. Many pastors, instead, begin with the preaching portion. However, if the congregation is inattentive, does not know what the passage means, what to look for in it, or cannot see its relevance to anything that is taking place in their lives, the congregation needs orientation; it is better to begin with the congregation. The object in doing so is to help them to approach the reading and exposition of the preaching portion with understanding and concern. The idea is to orient the congregation to the Scripture by showing its relevance to them.

Using the simplest form, a form that is useful when you recognize that there is already a high level of attention, understanding, and expectancy among the members of the congregation,[2] in the introduction you may make a statement, ask a question or series of questions, or both. Here are some samples of simple introductions:

1. *Assertion question:*

   "God gave each one of you certain gifts. How many of you are aware of this? Do you know what your gifts are? Well, today we shall take a close look at I Corinthians 12:6-8 to discover what God wants you to know about your gifts."[3]

2. *Question series:*

   "Are you a worrier? Have you ever prayed for peace and

2. Sometimes it is wise to have alternative introductions available when the state of the congregation cannot be predicted.

3. Notice how, at the outset, the sermon involves the congregation. Like the rest of the preaching outline, the introduction must be cast in the here-and-now, personalized preaching format. In the other samples you will find that the same thing holds true.

found that it didn't come? Have you tried to turn off that worry but couldn't find the switch? Yes? Well, let's take a fresh look at Philippians 4:6-9 to see if we can discover what has gone wrong.''

3. *Simple question:*

   ''How do you respond to trouble when it comes? Some complain, some whine, others get angry, and still others go to pieces. Obviously, these are all wrong, sinful responses. As we turn to Philippians 1:12-18 we shall see how God wants you to respond.''

4. *Simple statement:*

   ''Today, we are going to study what the Bible teaches about your sexuality.''[4]

This is the easiest, most direct, and quickest way to open a sermon. And it ought not to be disdained merely because it is so. However, there are some precautions to consider. In order to arrest attention, be sure that you

1. don't use this format in every sermon;
2. don't use it when there is little or no expectancy in the congregation;
3. don't use it when an explanation of one sort or another is in order.

When the congregation's attention and interest are likely to be difficult to attract and hold, use either a short story (children 9-99 years of age enjoy a story) or a startling statement. Let's begin with the latter. Here are two examples of a startling statement:

1. ''There is a murderer sitting in this congregation today.'' After this initial statement, a quick build-up of suspense, as the statement is enlarged and expanded, might follow: ''Yes, I mean it. Just yesterday he murdered someone. He didn't think

---

4. Some subjects, like this one, are their own interest-arousers. There is no need to elaborate; indeed, to do so may actually detract from attention and interest: the congregation wants you to get on with the subject, not to string out your information.

that anyone saw him, but he was wrong. I have a written statement from an eyewitness that I am going to read. Here is what it says: 'Everybody who hates his brother is a murderer' (I John 3:15).''

Obviously, you will want to use the startling statement with great care and infrequently. *How* you say what you say is so critical that you ought to write it out beforehand and insert it in your outline. Even the expansion should be written out, since this is the place where it is easiest to go wrong. Thus the introduction will appear in the outline as a short paragraph.

The frequency with which you use such an introduction, as well as how carefully it is worded, will have much to do with its effectiveness. If you cry "wolf, wolf" every week, the startling statement will quickly lose its effect. So, save this introduction for those occasions when you think you will need it—even when you know that you've come up with a doozie that you'd just love to use this week. Don't give in; scrap it. Use the startling statement *only when it will be needed,* i.e., only when it can be used purposefully.

The startling statement arouses a high level of attention at the very beginning that is difficult to sustain. So you must take great care about what immediately follows. It must not be a letdown; it must hold and deepen that interest. Probably it is wise in such a sermon, sustained from the outset on such a high emotional level, to fill it with punchy, short sentences, move rapidly from one point to the next, and close the sermon early. Short sermons, with a high level of emotional tension, probably make as much (or more) of an impact as longer, more deliberate and slower-moving ones. Keep it brief!

2. '' 'There is no hell; the whole idea is a scam devised by preachers and priests to hold congregations in line. The truth is, you might as well lie, steal, commit adultery, or do whatever you can get away with—God isn't really going to do anything about it.' That's what I heard a man say the other day. How would you answer him? How would you fortify your children against such teaching? And, by the way, is it possible that there is someone here today who is wondering whether what that man said may be right?''

That the startling statement is effective in arresting attention is without a doubt true. That it can be used only infrequently and only with great care in wording is also true.

A third way to open a sermon is with a brief story, example, or incident. This kind of introduction is self-explanatory and calls for no samples. But there are misuses connected with it against which some warnings quite appropriately may be issued. And a few remarks also may be made about how to use it most effectively. Discussion of the art of story-telling, using examples, etc., will be reserved for a later chapter.

First, never use a story that does not truly introduce. Sometimes we become enamored with a story or incident that we *want* to tell; so we use it even if it doesn't fit. *Never* do that. However, having said that, it might be helpful to state that there are ways of making a story, that at first didn't seem appropriate, quite fitting. One of these is to *contrast* it with what you wish to say. Something very desirable, great, etc., may be *set over against* the actual, existing situation. Another way is to alter the story: "That is what actually happened. But suppose, instead, it had happened like this. . . ."

Secondly, don't drag the story out too long. The purpose of the story is to capture the listener's attention and direct it toward the truth of the biblical passage; it is *not* to create interest in the story itself, for itself. Be sure that the story leads the listener's mind to the message; if it doesn't it distracts and leads *away* from the message. These two misuses (apart from problems connected with story-telling *per se*) are the greatest problems connected with story-telling in introductions that I know.

To use the short story, example, or incident effectively, use dialogue and descriptive color if the story is to be extended to any length (see information on this *infra*). But carefully think through what, precisely, is *necessary* in the telling of the story to make the point you wish to make and then peel away everything else—no matter how tantalizing it may seem to be. In the introduction, economy is of the essence.

Also, be sure not only that the story makes the point, or can be used to do so, but also that it involves or can be used to involve the congregation. There are three basic ways in which you can do this:

1. Tell a story about the congregation itself.
2. Tell a story about something or someone in which the congregation is interested.
3. Tell a story, and then at its conclusion, *in one sentence,* apply it to the congregation (e.g., "And, that's exactly what has been happening here," or "Don't think that such things take place only in New York or other large cities. *Your* child. . . .")

There are a number of secondary purposes for using a story, but I cannot enter into them here. All that needs to be said in this place is that these must always be subjected to the major purpose of the story in an introduction—to arrest attention and create interest by involving the congregation in the subject of the message.

While introductions may occur to you at any time during the preparation of a sermon, usually they are most easily and best developed when all else has been roughed in. Then, and perhaps then only, will you know exactly what you will be introducing. When preparing the introduction, consider whether in some way you can tie it in with the conclusion. This wraps up the entire sermon in a way that gives it unity and force (e.g., "So you see, the problem we raised at the beginning has been solved. . . ." or "Now, if you will only do what you have learned today, just let that man [the one mentioned in the introduction] come into our midst. You'll be ready for him"").

Introductions are important, as you can see. But so are conclusions, to which we must now turn our attention.

Class Assignments:

1. Discover three good introductions in existing sermons and, in a three-page paper, discuss what makes them good.
2. Produce five good introductions of your own to hand in.

11

PURPOSEFUL
CONCLUSIONS

Without a good conclusion, the (otherwise) best sermon is a dud. As we have seen, introductions are important; if anything, conclusions are even more important. But conclusions raise different issues.

Like introductions, conclusions take their cue from the *telos* of the sermon proper. If, in the body of the sermon, primarily you have been teaching new truths, in the conclusion you will probably want to restate and reemphasize these. A summary of what was taught will be helpful, but it should be brief and should focus only on the major thrusts that were made. One caution: be sure not to introduce new material when summarizing. If you want to use such material, go back and see where it best fits in the sermon body and insert it there.

However, you may restate the old material in new ways. But the new way (or any old one that is reiterated in the conclusion) must be the way in which you want the truth or truths to be remembered. What you say in the conclusion is what people usually take away with them. This fact alone shows you how vital the conclusion—and its form—can be.

The conclusion should truly conclude. Another way of saying that is that there should be only one conclusion. Some preachers are in their final approach toward the runway when, at an altitude of only a few feet from the ground, they get a new thought and—instead of landing—zoom up into the air again. Then, once more, they circle the field, line up with the landing strip, lower their flaps and start to come in for a landing, only to shoot up into the sky instead. Or, to change the figure, some preachers are musical composers who, like Gershwin in his "An American in Paris," tease the listener into thinking they are concluding the piece when they are not. Multiple conclusions destroy sermons and discourage congregations. There are other preachers who, instead of concluding, simply stop abruptly, and still others who merely fade away. Some weasel out of the sermon with a statement like, "Now, may God bless these words to each of you," and there is a class that stumble around looking for a way out, repeating and repeating themselves until they see any sort of opening and then make a dash for it. All these problems stem from a failure to take the time to prepare conclusions ahead of time.

Conclusions vary in specific purpose, but again, the purpose of the conclusion is directly related to and dictated by the *telic* thrust of the preaching portion. That must always be kept in mind. As I have indicated earlier, the *telic* statement at the head of the outline and the conclusion should match. The former should state the destination to which the preacher intends to travel, and in the latter he should have arrived and be speaking about the main thing he found when he got there.

The conclusion either summarizes, applies, or implements truth, or, as in most instances, does some or all of the above. Surely it is important to preach for results—the results that the Holy Spirit intended when He caused the preaching portion to be written. It is in the conclusion that the appeal to "believe" or "go" or "do" something or other is made.

Some preachers conclude weakly with a verse of poetry or a line or two from a hymn. Rarely is this effective. Someone else's writing breaks the continuity of *your* message. His style—especially if it is in meter and rhyme—jars with yours. The poetic piece hardly ever says *exactly* what you want to say and usually is somewhat out of kilter with the *telos* of the passage. And, even in those rare instances in which the fit is fairly snug, most poetry is weak because it is more contemplative than persuasive.

And, while we are at it, let me condemn outright the singing of a hymn following the sermon. If the conclusion has been well thought out, and has been effectively delivered, then the congregation should be left with that to think about. It is unwise to risk doing anything that might mar or dissipate the effect of the conclusion. Probably as much harm has been done to good sermons through the desultory words and ill-suited music of a concluding hymn as by any other single factor. It is weak preachers, whose sermons do not have powerful conclusions, who do something else to try to redeem the morning or evening effort, to whom these final hymns belong.

Good conclusions, like good sermons, then, work toward the goal of achieving the *telos* of the sermon. Often, if the introduction was right to the point, the conclusion can be made in terms of the introduction itself, thus wrapping up the entire sermon in one bow:

> "When we began, I asked if you knew what to do if someone challenged your faith. Now. . . ."

Using a story as the conclusion to a sermon, now and then, can be effective but is difficult to pull off well. If not done properly, if the story does not do *exactly* what you wish it to do, if it does not have precisely the same tone and warmth that is appropriate to the mood you have established, it will *detract* rather than help. Until you learn all the principles of story-telling, and all that you need to know about the purposes of conclusions and how to realize them, and learn them well, it will be unwise to try to conclude a sermon with a story. For this reason, among others, you will discover that even the greatest preachers rarely use them. But Jesus did in the Sermon on the Mount.

Stories are best used to concretize and to apply truth. Because they personalize truth and integrate it into life and action, they can pack an emotional wallop that drives home the *telos* with force. Consider the following:

> . . . So, you have learned that God provides not only the wis-

dom but the strength and know-how to do His will.

One day a small child decided to make his daddy a birthday present. Having gathered the saw, the rasp, some sandpaper, screws, and a screwdriver together, he called, "Daddy, will you come here and show me how to begin?" Again and again, he asked for help. The patient father gladly gave instruction and offered suggestions. When the gift was completed, it was the result of a combined effort; the child made it, but he couldn't have done so without his daddy's help at every point.

Do you think that the father received his birthday present with any less joy for knowing that without his help it could not have been made? Do you think that he thought any the less of it because the tools and materials were his? Of course he didn't! He joyously, proudly received his son's gift. So, too, will your heavenly Father graciously receive the works of your hands—even though you and He both know that without Him you could have done nothing. He loves to help His children; ask Him for what *you* need—right now, as we bow in prayer.

The simplest way of concluding a message is with a series of appeals, made either in the form of a command cluster ("Serve Him. Serve Him today. Serve Him with love; with all your heart, and soul, and strength") or as a question cluster (Won't you listen to the plea of your brother or sister, as Christ commands? Will you be reconciled to him or her? Won't you forgive and seek forgiveness for your own sin, right now, at the conclusion of this sermon, or as soon as possible? Or, will you force him to resort to further steps in church discipline?").

Often, some sort of concluding implementation is useful (if not necessary):[1]

> There may be any number of acceptable ways of putting this biblical command into action.[2] If you can think of a better one that falls within the area of biblical principle, good. But if you are committed to getting started right away, as you should be, and don't know how to begin, let me suggest one way. First, . . .

1. I shall have more to say about implementation later on.
2. Be careful to distinguish between the absoluteness of a divine command and the implementation of it, which, if not absolutized in the passage, must be set forth as no more than a biblically directed suggestion.

Of course, the implementation itself, while forming the bulk of the conclusion, will be rounded off with (no more than) one or two concluding sentences.

The purpose of the conclusion, then, is not merely to bring the sermon to an end. It does that. But the principal function that it serves is to capsulize and capitalize on the sermon *telos*. The listener goes away with the conclusion, which always calls for some change on his part, in mind. It must be powerful. Weak conclusions leave the impression, rightly or wrongly, that the whole message was weak.

Because true sermons always call for change, often decision-making takes place when they are being preached, most frequently during the conclusion. A preacher must realize that this is likely to happen, acknowledge the fact, and plan for it when preparing conclusions. While a pastor certainly is not a salesman making a pitch, like a salesman he is speaking for results. Both are out to accomplish something. It would be foolish for the salesman to explain all about his product and then fail to ask the prospective customer to purchase it. That is why he "closes" or "draws the net." Many salesmen today use unethical or questionable tactics in doing so; obviously anything even slightly bordering on this must be avoided. But after all precautions have been taken, there remains a biblical obligation to "urge," "persuade," "encourage," and "authoritatively instruct" (cf. the pastoral epistles) the listener to believe and do whatever God commands.

This last point leads to the heated discussion of invitations in evangelistic preaching.

Class Assignments:

1. Choose five good conclusions from printed sermons representing five different approaches. Discuss the strengths of each and what you think made the particular approach used appropriate and effective in that sermon. The report should be no longer than five pages.
2. Be ready to present a conclusion of your own in class.

12

EVANGELISTIC INVITATIONS

Earlier, I noted that preaching is of two sorts: evangelistic and edificational. Evangelism in the Scriptures is done ''out there,'' where the unbelieving are, not primarily in the services of the church. Of course, the gospel relates to everything else that is preached, and no sermon—even in a basically edificational setting—ever should be preached unless it is related to the good news. But that fact does not mean that in edificational preaching only (or even primarily) the gospel should be preached. In evangelistic preaching, the gospel is dominant; in edificational preaching the focus is on the implications of the gospel for the lives of believers.

That this preaching of the gospel even in edificational contexts in biblical times was recognized as ''standard operational procedure'' is apparent from I Corinthians 14:23-25:

> If, then, when the whole church comes together everybody is speaking in other languages and ungifted persons or unbelievers enter the meeting, won't they say you are crazy? But if everybody is prophesying and some unbeliever or ungifted one enters, he will be convicted by all and judged by all, the things hidden in his heart will be disclosed, and as a result falling down on his face he will worship God and declare that God is really among you.

Here, clearly, the possibility of the conversion of an unbeliever in an edificational context is contemplated, and even described. But that still doesn't stamp the Bible's approval on turning what should be edificational preaching into evangelistic preaching, as some do.

However, there are times when it is appropriate to preach evangelistic sermons. Certainly, in an advertised week of "special services" it would be appropriate to preach only the gospel (how productive these meetings will be in attracting unbelievers may vary from region to region). If the local Boy Scout troop should visit your church on "Boy Scout Sunday," that would be a good time to preach an evangelistic sermon in a normally edificational context. And, of course, there are any number of other occasions when a pastor may "do the work of an evangelist," not only in pastoral counseling, but in his preaching outside of the edificational service of the congregation. The question that arises is whether, in these situations, some specialized form of conclusion, incorporating an "invitation" or "altar call" is proper.

First, let me say that all sorts of conclusions in evangelistic contexts (questions, commands, stories, etc.) should contain a clear restatement of the gospel and should call upon the unbeliever to trust Christ for salvation. The plain statement of the gospel will place before the unbeliever precisely what it is that he is being commanded to believe.

The good news, or gospel, is set forth in unmistakable terms in I Corinthians 15:1-4):

> Now I want to remind you, brothers, of the good news that I announced to you, which indeed you received, in which you stand, through which also you are saved, if you hold on to the message of the good news that I announced to you (unless your faith was empty). I delivered to you as of greatest importance what I also received, that Christ died for our sins, in agreement with the Scriptures, and that He was buried, and that He was raised on the third day in agreement with the Scriptures, . . .

Because there are many—even preachers—who seem fuzzy about what the good news is, note that Paul says that there are two Old

Testament predictions, fulfilled in Christ, that constitute the good news:

1. His sacrificial, substitutionary, penal death;
2. His bodily resurrection from the dead.

That it was this message which the early church proclaimed is demonstrated in the New Testament treatise on evangelism, the Book of Acts. From beginning to end, whenever witness is borne, personally or publicly, the death and resurrection of Christ are at the center of that proclamation (cf. 2:23, 24; 3:13-15; 4:10; 5:29-32; 10:39-41; 13:28-33[1]).

1. ". . . this Man, delivered up by God's predetermined foreknowledge, by the hands of lawless men, you killed by crucifixion! But God resurrected Him, releasing Him from the agonies of death, because it wasn't possible for Him to be held by it" (Acts 2:23, 24).

". . . The God of Abraham, Isaac and Jacob, the God of our fathers, glorified His Servant Jesus, Whom you delivered over and denied in front of Pilate when he had decided to free Him. But you denied the Holy and Righteous One and asked for a murderer to be given to you. So you killed the Author of life, Whom God raised from the dead, to which fact we are witnesses" (Acts 3:13-15).

". . . let all of you and all of the people of Israel know that it is by the name of Jesus Christ the Nazarene, Whom you crucified, Whom God raised from the dead, by Him this person stands before you a well man" (Acts 4:10).

"Peter and the apostles said, 'We must obey God rather than men. Our fathers' God raised Jesus, Whom you killed by hanging Him on a tree. God exalted this Man to a place at His right hand as a Ruler and Savior to give repentance and forgiveness of sins to Israel. And we are witnesses of these things, and so is the Holy Spirit that God gave to those who obey Him' " (Acts 5:29-32).

". . . And we are witnesses of everything that He did in the Jews' country and in Jerusalem. They killed Him by hanging Him on a tree, but God raised Him up on the third day and had Him appear, not to all the people, but to us who were previously chosen by God to be witnesses. We ate and drank with Him after He rose from the dead" (Acts 10:39-41).

". . . And though they could find no grounds for His death, they asked Pilate to destroy Him. And when they had finished doing everything that was written about Him, they took Him down from the tree and laid Him in a tomb. But God raised Him from the dead, and for many days He appeared to those who came up with Him from Galilee to Jerusalem, who now are His witnesses to the people. And we announce to you the good news that what God promised to the fathers, He has fulfilled to us, their children, by raising Jesus as it is written in the second Psalm: 'You are My Son; today I have become Your Father' " (Acts 13:28-33).

The gospel must be proclaimed in evangelism, or listeners will not know what to believe. But it must also be proclaimed properly. It must never be preached as an "add on," or as an adjunct to what one already has said, the way that one adds a new appliance to his house. Exactly not that. The gospel is preached together with a call to repentance (*metanoia*=a change of mind, about God, Christ, and one's self). The gospel isn't added on; it comes with the impact that turns everything else inside out. All wrong thoughts about God as One who will allow sin to go unpunished, about Christ as merely a good man and a religious leader, and about one's own worth and merit must be scrapped. Instead, the listener must acknowledge his own sin and guilt, that he stands condemned before a holy God who will punish unforgiven sinners in hell, and that Christ is the God-man who came in flesh to die in the stead of guilty sinners. By faith he must believe that Christ died for his sins and confess Him as Lord (Rom. 10:9, 10).

This good news—that all who depend on Christ as Savior will be saved—must be preached to all alike; there is a free and universal offer of the gospel in which all must be called upon to believe (Acts 17:30). It is not the preacher's task to single out some to whom he will preach the gospel while by-passing others; his task is to proclaim the Word to all. Of course, only those whose hearts the Lord opens (Acts 16:14[2]) will believe; but it is God's task, not ours, to determine who they are. Like Paul, we are to speak to all (v. 13).

Evangelistic preaching in the New Testament, as in this case (v. 15), seems to have been followed up by an invitation—to be *baptized*. That pattern was set forth in Matthew 28:18-20,[3] and was followed

2. "On the Sabbath we went outside the gate to a place by a river, where we expected to find a place of prayer. And we sat down and spoke to the women who had gathered there. A woman named Lydia, from the city of Thyatira, who sold purple goods and was a worshiper of God, heard, and the Lord opened her heart to pay attention to what Paul said. When she and her household were baptized, she urged us this way: 'If you have determined that I am faithful to the Lord, come and stay at my house.' And she prevailed upon us to do so" (Acts 16:13-15).

3. "And Jesus went to them and said to them, 'All authority in heaven and on earth has been given to Me. Go, therefore, and make disciples from all nations, baptizing them into the Name of the Father and of the Son and of the Holy Spirit, teaching them

consistently throughout the Book of Acts. Consider some examples:

> Then those who received his message were baptized, and about
> three thousand persons were added that day (Acts 2:41).

Note especially the words "added that day" in the passage just quoted. The baptism of those who believed took place "that day" and "added" them to the existing company of believers. Consider also Acts 8:38:

> Then he ordered the chariot to stop, and they both went down to
> the water, both Philip and the eunuch, and he baptized him.

Once again the pattern holds; the Ethiopian eunuch believed, they stopped the chariot and—on the spot, at the first convenient place—he was baptized. Once more:

> And he took them in that very hour of the night and washed their
> stripes, and he and all his family were baptized right away (Acts
> 16:33).

Don't miss the words, "in that very hour" and "right away," in the passage. It seems to have been the regular practice of ministers of the Word to baptize persons into the company of the faithful *as soon as possible*.

Probably our own, modern substitutes for this—raising hands, coming forward, etc.—are the result of a felt need to do something for those who believe. It seems certain that those who believed were distinguished from those who did not. There is no evidence that New Testament evangelistic preachers asked them to come forward, but there is every indication that they did invite those who believed to be baptized:

> And Peter said to them, "Repent and be baptized, each one of you
> on the basis of the name of Jesus Christ for the forgiveness of your
> sins, and you will receive the gift of the Holy Spirit (Acts 2:38).

And it seems that this was the way in which new converts professed

---

to observe all that I have commanded you; and remember, I will be with you always,
to the close of the age' " (Matt. 28:18-20).

their faith in Christ and came under the care and discipline of the church.

At this point, let me make it absolutely clear that baptism does not save and that baptism is not a part of the gospel itself, as some erroneously affirm. Paul unmistakably distinguishes between the gospel and baptism in I Corinthians 1:17 when he writes: "Christ didn't send me to baptize but to preach the good news." Baptism is not a means of salvation, but a means for proclaiming openly that one has been converted and united to Christ and wishes to identify himself with His church (see my book, *The Meaning and Mode of Baptism,*[4] for more on the subject).

It seems to me that it is time that we stopped arguing over "invitations" to come forward, etc., and began working out the ways and means of following the New Testament pattern. If we became more biblical in this respect, we would solve most of the questions now being debated about "invitations."

There is another matter, often confused with "giving the invitation": speaking to inquirers after a sermon. This matter is settled by Paul's example in Acts 13:43:

> When the congregation broke up, many of the Jews and of the worshiping proselytes followed Paul and Barnabas, who spoke to them and urged them to persevere by God's grace.

To invite inquirers to remain afterwards to talk further, therefore, seems quite proper. That means that on the day when the Boy Scouts make their appearance, it certainly would not be amiss to publicly state in conclusion something like this:

> If any of you here has trusted Christ as your Savior during this sermon, I urge you to identify yourself following the service so that we may follow up on what you have done and help you to get started properly in your new life [a part of that follow-up would be making sure that the gospel is clear to all converts and that they are confronted with their need to profess their faith and to submit to the care and discipline of Christ's church by baptism].

4. Phillipsburg, N.J.: Presbyterian and Reformed Publishing Co.

Moreover, you might invite anyone who has questions about the gospel also to remain and speak further with the pastor or elders.

"Why don't we use baptism in connection with evangelism as they did in the New Testament?" There are a number of answers to that question: tradition, eliminating denominational differences in inter-denominational "campaigns," etc. But there is one other reason: we do not receive ("add") converts to the body by baptism "right away" because we have virtually abandoned church discipline in our churches today. We think we must "prove" converts first; after all, "What if they turn out to be unbelievers?" The New Testament exhibits no such apprehension over this possibility because there was a means of handling that contingency (cf. Matt. 18:15ff.). New Testament evangelists make it easy to get into the church "that very hour," but they also make it mean something to stay in. We, in contrast, make it (somewhat) hard to get in, but once in the body a member usually is secure for life regardless of his beliefs or lifestyle. It is easier to remain a member of the average church today than it is to continue one's membership in a lodge! If we exercised biblical care and discipline, we would have little or no difficulty in adopting and following the biblical pattern.

The answer, then, to the question of invitations or no invitations is: *"Give a biblical invitation* to profess faith in Christ and be added to the number in baptism."[5] This invitation may be issued, as Peter issued it, in the evangelistic message, usually as a part of its conclusion.

That the New Testament preachers gave this gospel message with a sort of urgency ("Believe *now"*) seems apparent not only from the Book of Hebrews, in which the recurring theme, "Today, if you hear His voice, don't harden your hearts," appears, but also from the policy of Paul and his companions in Acts when they turned from those who would not believe and when they issued an urgent warning:

5. Throughout I have been assuming that the evangelistic preaching is being done outside of a covenant context. That means that, unlike covenant children, those to whom one is preaching are not members of the visible body or under its care and discipline.

And Paul and Barnabas, speaking boldly, said, "It was necessary to speak God's Word to you first. Since you thrust it away and don't consider yourselves worthy of eternal life, we are turning to the Gentiles" (Acts 13:46).

"So then, watch out that what the prophets spoke about doesn't come upon you: 'See you scoffers; wonder and perish because I will work a work in your days—a work that you simply won't believe if somebody tells you about it' " (Acts 13:40, 41).

Evangelistic preaching, then, issued an urgent call for action and, when it was heeded, responded immediately ("in that very hour," "right away"). New Testament evangelists seem never to have preached the gospel in the abstract, take-it-or-leave-it fashion we sometimes encounter today. They preached with a purpose: to achieve the *telos* of the Holy Spirit. In evangelism, the immediate *telos* of any evangelistic passage is the conversion of those who will believe the gospel.

Class Assignments:

1. In a paper of major length, study and discuss the New Testament evidence for baptizing converts at the end of an evangelistic sermon. Be sure to consider those biblical references which are not mentioned in this chapter.
2. Consider the practical problems that might be connected with reintroducing the biblical practice into churches today. Be prepared to discuss this in class. You may wish to write out a proposal about this that you would want to make to a congregation when you become its pastor.

PURPOSEFUL PLANNING

In various places in earlier chapters I have frequently referred to the idea of a study-planning-and-preparation program in which you will be able to prepare sermons six months in advance. The following article, which appeared in *The Journal of Pastoral Practice* 3, 3:161, and later in a book of essays on preaching, *Truth Apparent,* tells the whole story. I shall quote it in full:

Most pastors enjoy preaching. Moreover, many thoroughly enjoy the hours of preparation spent in the study among their commentaries, etc., in the work of biblical exposition and sermon preparation. Why, then, do we hear so much dissatisfaction about preaching from preachers themselves these days?

The basic dissatisfaction, about which I am speaking, is the outgrowth of another problem stemming (in turn) from still another.

First, dissatisfaction comes from not "having enough time" to prepare properly. It is precisely that opportunity which pastors enjoy so much that is lacking. They *want* to spend more time in the study of the Word and in the preparation of messages, but other demands constantly call them away from this work. Doing half-baked study and inadequate preparation is what takes away the joy of preaching. That's the first problem.

But before going on to the second problem (from which it derives), let's consider this matter of the lack of time a bit more thoroughly. Perhaps you are expecting me to say, "Well, if you're too busy to find time, then you're just too busy." There is something to that, of course. Any number of preachers take on tasks that do not belong to them; disregarding the clear statement of their function in Ephesians 4:11, 12, they try to do the work of their people for them, in addition to all their own. That, of course, is impossible. Some pastors run a taxi service, mow lawns, operate mimeograph machines, etc., when there are any number of persons in the congregation who could (should) do these things instead. When they arrogate to themselves the tasks that others ought to do, but are not doing, they make it easy for others to shirk their responsibilities, they rob them of their blessings, and they crowd out the study of Scripture and sermon preparation. It ought to be a rule for every pastor not to do anything himself that a member of his congregation can do (or can be taught to do) as well as (or better than) he can. Of course, there will be times (in emergencies, in brand new mission churches, etc.) when a pastor must do such things, but he will not make it a practice. His work is ministering the Word, privately and publicly, in order to build up and encourage all the members of the flock to pursue their own ministries. When *extraneous* activities are eliminated from his schedule, he will have more time for study and sermon preparation.

"But that isn't all," you say. Right! I know there are weeks that we'd all like to forget; and I know that they come more frequently than we'd like to think. On Monday it looks tight (especially with that special men's meeting address on Saturday night), but everything seems to be in hand. You have selected your preaching portions for Sunday morning and evening and the prayer meeting topic, and you are about to go to work on them (preparation for Saturday night will have to wait till Thursday). You are well into your exegesis by Tuesday morning, when things begin to break loose. The phone—that two-faced blessing and curse—rings. Mrs. Green has been rushed to the hospital . . . it is serious . . . can you come immediately? You do, of course (torn at leaving the study at such a time). When you get back (three hours later), there is the afternoon's list of activities staring you in the face. No way for you to fudge on them. So, you don't. That means one half of a morning's study shot. "I'll catch up tonight," you think, as you drive out of the yard. But that night finds you at the hospital again—Mrs. Green has taken a turn for worse; they think she may die. Somehow, she rallies, and you go home late, weary, but no further ahead in your study. Wednesday morning. Sunday sermons are set aside. Tonight's prayer meeting must be considered. "I'll take off this afternoon and do the study I had hoped to do yesterday. Who is that driving up to the study? Bill and Jane Wilkes. Wonder what they want?" It turns out that last night Jane threatened to leave Bill, and only at the last minute was she persuaded to stay *on condition that they see the pastor right away.* "Of course," you hear yourself saying, "sit down; let's talk about it." Glad to help, but reluctant to give up the time, you counsel them. When you are through, an hour and a half later, your secretary informs you that this *really* looks like it for Mrs. Green—and that the family would like to see you (they have all gathered together at the hospital). You go (of course!). Mrs. Green dies (this means another unanticipated message for Saturday morning at the funeral). Bill and Jane take up another day or two—and so it goes (I'll not finish out the week—it's too discouraging to do so). I know about those kinds of weeks—and what they can do to sermon preparation and study.

"Well?" you ask. "What can I do about that sort of problem? There isn't any way that you can regulate funerals, marriages breaking up, etc., so that they fit your study schedule, is there?" Don't be too sure! While you can't predict emergencies, you may be able to regulate your schedule to fit emergencies in a way that doesn't destroy your study and preparation.

I am about to make a suggestion that at first you will reject—but hear me out. In one fell swoop you can solve not only the problem of weekly pressure, but a number of other problems as well. Indeed, following this suggestion can—as it did for me in my last pastorate— make preaching a pleasure.

The suggestion is simple, but profound: prepare every sermon six months in advance. Now wait, don't turn me off. Hear me out, I beg you. I want to make it clear that this is really practical—the most practical thing to do. Here are my reasons:

1. You gain plenty of lead-time that will allow you to make all the schedule adjustments that you need to meet emergencies. What you lose in time one week can be gained the next week (or even the week after).
2. You gain perspective on your text. Too many sermons are cut down green; they do not have time to ripen.
3. Illustrations come naturally. When you know well in advance what you will be preaching about, all the general reading you do, as well as the experiences you have, feed into the sermon. You don't have to *search* for examples; they *come* to you.
4. When preaching a series of sermons on a book, you can preach the first sermon in the light of the exegesis of the entire book. Instead of discovering that what you preached in the first chapter was wrong (now that you understand it in terms of what is said later, in chapter 3), you begin to preach the book only after having studied the whole.
5. You solve the problems of an exegetical conscience. When you begin preparing a message on Monday or Tuesday before it is to be preached, you may move along swimmingly until—in the mail Friday—you receive that new commentary you ordered, which knocks your previous understanding of the passage into the proverbial hat. Now, what do you do? There isn't any time to adequately prepare a *new* sermon. Do you preach the old one, knowing it is wrong? I'm afraid many do.
6. Preachers tend to ride hobbies (Ezekiel at night, Revelation in the morning, and Daniel for prayer meeting). Planning large blocks of sermons, well in advance, requires thought about balanced feeding of the flock. You see the bigger picture.

All in all, then, I think you can see the values of preparing six months in advance.

"Sure, but how do I do that?"

What you do is this:

1. You do the exegesis for your passage and outline it in rough form six months ahead.
2. You allow time for your thinking about it to mature, gathering illustrations, etc.
3. A couple of weeks before preaching you pull out your folder and put the sermon into final form.

Of course, you can always make adjustments in unforeseen circumstances by inserting a special sermon now and then to meet these.

Let me diagram the process (see next page):

"OK, OK. I can see the value of this. But is it practical? Can it really be done? If so, how?"

What you are now doing isn't practical, is it? Well then, consider this.

1. The best time to make the change is when changing pastorates. Simply preach out of the barrel for six months while preparing the next six. A sermon is best preached the third or fourth time!
2. If you are in seminary, determine not to leave with less than six months' sermons in hand. Start out right from the beginning.[1]
3. If you are in a pastorate, and intend to stay, but want to switch over to the new program, I suggest this:
   a. Dig into the barrel for your oldest, very first sermons.
   b. Develop six months worth of sermons from these.
   c. Use each major point of these old sermons as a separate sermon in itself. (Typically, new preachers include too much in their sermons. When you preach these points separately, you will have the sermons you should have had to begin with.)

I have outlined a process and procedure that can revolutionize your preaching. Don't lay it aside lightly. I have suggested this to any number of persons. Those who have adopted it agree that they have

---

1. A seminary course, designed for this purpose, would be extremely valuable to students.

been liberated. Preaching can be the pleasure you always wanted it to be.

The Preaching Year

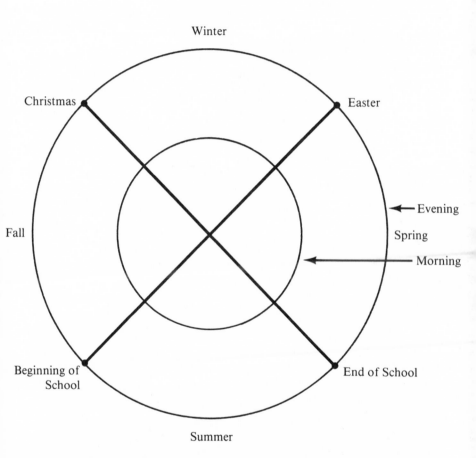

You divide the year (roughly) into four segments, according to some functional form (as suggested above). Then you plan two segments of the year all at one time (e.g., at the end of summer you might plan the spring and summer segments of the following year.

Then you begin studying each of the messages to be preached during those segments, keeping six months ahead. That looks like this:

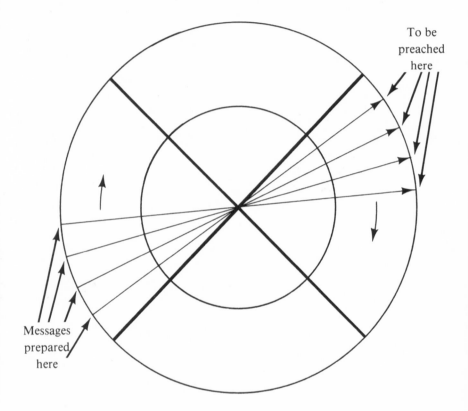

As you can see, there are many decided advantages to following this program. Of course, someone ought to have told you years ago, but he didn't. You must now replace present habits with new ones. That will not be easy, but I guarantee it will be worthwhile. I have now told you, and I urge you to make the change. Give it a try for one year (two six-month planning sessions) and you will never want to revert to the old ways again.

The two segments ahead also can be prepared in balanced terms by using the diagram, thus:

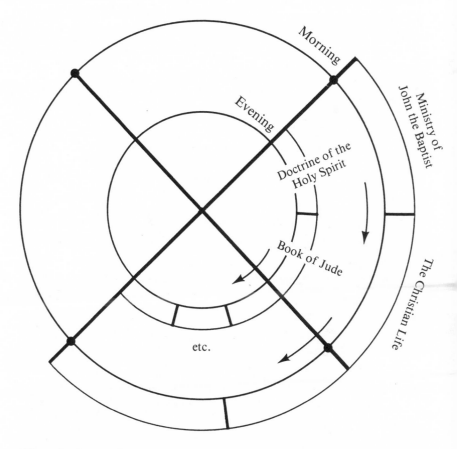

Class Assignments:

1. If you have no course to prepare you for your first six months, determine how you can plan ahead on your own (using the results of exegetical courses, etc.) and write out a proposal for yourself (to be handed in).
2. Visit with four preachers. Discuss their study-planning programs. Tell them about this one. In a brief report tell what you discovered.

SENSE
APPEAL

The immediate purpose of using sense appeal in preaching is to add the dimension of reality to truth by helping listeners to sense (experience) what you are teaching from the Scriptures. Sense stimulation in preaching enables listeners to "live" or "relive" an event or experience. There is a great difference between merely thinking about something and experiencing it. Thinking *about* it means there is a significant emotional distance *from* it; experiencing it means there is a cold chill that runs up your spine when it comes to mind. Of course, thinking is necessary to experiencing and may lead to it (a person can think himself into a panic). But, in a preaching context, many listeners *on their own never* experience anything unless the preacher helps them.

To experience an event in preaching is to enter into that event so fully that the emotions appropriate to that event are felt, just as if one were actually going through it. When a preacher says what he relates in such a way that he stimulates one or more of the five senses, thus triggering emotion, then the listener may be said to "experience" the event. In that way, the event will become "real" to him, which means it has become concretized (or personalized), memorable, and, in the fullest sense of the word, understandable.

All that I shall have to say about sense appeal in the remainder of this chapter is a two-edged sword that cuts both listener and preacher. That is because of the fundamental dynamic in preaching: in order to move others, the preacher himself must be moved. If he wishes his congregation to experience the truth, he must first experience it when studying it and then, again, when preaching it. That means he must be free enough to allow the truth to affect him as he preaches.[1]

The deeper purpose of sense appeal, with its arousal of emotions, lending their dimension of reality to what is said, is full—including experiential—understanding. Sense appeal, when effective, helps the members to experience the impact of truth in addition to merely thinking about it. The Scriptures, and scriptural principles, come alive for them and help motivate them to a biblical response.

Without exception, every great preacher has cultivated and learned to use skillfully the power of sense appeal. For the study of the use of sense appeal by one such preacher, see my *Sense Appeal in the Sermons of Charles Haddon Spurgeon* (Presbyterian and Reformed Publishing Co.).

Most homiletics books speak about "illustrating"[2] truth and making it "vivid." But those terms refer to communication by means of appeal to but a single sense: the sense of sight. That failure, so inherent in the very single sense vocabulary of homiletics, has led to dull, lifeless preaching. Of course, there are many dull, lifeless preachers for whom it is difficult to "paint word pictures" that appeal to the sense of sight, let alone learn to help congregations to taste, touch, smell, and even hear with the ear. Even though the preacher works in the medium of sound, few preachers, when preaching, ever make sounds, refer to sounds, or trigger the memory of sounds in the listener's mind. These preachers are like dull textbooks rather than like lively events. If they attempt sense appeal at all, they attempt to touch the listener's emotions through an appeal to the sense of sight

---

1. Occasionally this will mean shedding a tear, but it should never be allowed to go so far as to make communication impossible.
2. To illustrate this, literally, "to light up" or "brighten."

alone. But if you wish to communicate biblical truth effectively, without squeezing it dry, you must learn, rather, to appeal to the full range of human senses as the Bible itself does. In no other way can you help your congregation to experience truth as the Scriptures set it forth.

Fundamentally, emotions may be aroused by sense appeal through the use of

1. evocative language,
2. storytelling (sometimes called "illustrating"),
3. sound, and
4. gestures and other bodily actions.

Let's take a look at these.

Evocative Words

I shall discuss style (language usage) later on, so for now we shall limit ourselves to but one aspect of style: the use of evocative (or emotion-arousing) words. And, we shall look at these solely in relationship to sense appeal. Of course, the words themselves have no evocative power; what is evocative in one context (or for one person) may not be evocative in another (or for another person). Indeed, the same word may evoke opposite responses from different people. Say the word "Bible" to an avowed atheist like Madeline Murray O'Hare and to Jerry Falwell and you will discover the difference. The word "gentile" in the context of Acts 22 was definitely a highly evocative term; used in Romans 15:16, it would have been far less so.

Because of this varying evocativeness of words according to context and audience, it is impossible to list words according to their evocative character. Any word, as Benjamin Franklin observed when commenting on Whitefield's ability to bring tears by speaking the word "Mesopotamia," can be made evocative; similarly, any seemingly evocative term can be used non-evocatively. Everything depends on context and manner (we shall consider manner in a later chapter).

The preacher, then, must be careful about his use of words that may arouse emotions when he doesn't want them aroused or the wrong ones aroused. Again, he must be aware of what effect the occasion and the attitude of the congregation may have upon his use of words. He must learn to select a suit from among his more formal suits of words when speaking at a funeral, just as he will wear his most informal word-clothing at the young people's weiner roast.

Evocative words appeal to the senses, stir emotion, and bring about other responses. When speaking of frying bacon and eggs, one man's choice of words will do little more than conjure up a vague image, while the words of a second will cause the listener not only to hear the bacon crackling and spitting in the pan, but virtually make his mouth water as the listener can practically sniff the aroma too! One preacher describes a scene in which people are relaxing after a hard day's work; that's about as far as it goes. When another does so, his congregation can "feel" their sore limbs and swollen hands as well as the glorious sensation that arises when one stretches his weary arms over his head.

Look at how Proverbs 26:13-15 describes the sluggard:

> The sluggard says, "There's a lion in the road! There's a lion in the streets!"

Just listen to him make his exaggerated, full-of-holes excuses! You can almost hear his tone of voice; can't you see his assumed expression of fear or concern? Proverbs continues:

> As the door turns on its hinges. . . .

See how slowly it moves? Hear it squeak?

> . . . so does a sluggard on his bed.

He's even too lazy to turn over quickly! And now, comes this fine description:

> The sluggard buries his hand in the dish; it tires him to return it to his mouth.[3]

Can't you see him just languishing at the breakfast table with a hand in his bowl of oatmeal, too lazy to raise it to his mouth to eat? That is evocative writing! You can "feel" the sluggard's every motion.

3. Berkeley version.

Proverbs is full of such material. Feel this one:

As a thorn goes up into the hand. . . .

"Ouch!" you say. But no, notice this nice twist: the hand in question
is anesthetized by alcohol:

. . . of a drunkard, so is a proverb in the mouth of fools.[4]

The proverb in question makes no impact because the person who
speaks it is insensitive to its meaning as is a drunkard to the pain of a
thorn.

Make a study of Proverbs 25–28, concentrating on the evocative
use of words, and you will learn a lot about how to appeal to men
through *all* their senses. You will discover that in these chapters
Solomon appeals to all five senses: e.g., 25:11, 12: the sense of sight;
25:13, 19: the tactile sense; 25:16: the sense of taste; 25:21: the sense
of hearing; 26:11: the sense of smell. The feelings of pain, cold, heat,
nausea, pleasure, anger, irritation, sorrow, frustration, weariness,
fear, etc., may all be found there. And all this and more in brief,
one- or two-sentence proverbs! Think how much can be done in a
paragraph.

The man who speaks abstractly and dully, rather than concretely
and evocatively, must be spending too much time reading dull
materials and too little reading the Bible. Evocative language, the
language of sense appeal, is the language of the Bible.

Storytelling

Evocative language is useful not only in writing proverbs but also
in telling stories. But stories add quite a few other factors that tend
to make them even more effective in appealing to the senses.
Therefore you must learn to "illustrate" your sermons (I shall use
the word "storytelling" for "illustrating," since the latter is a
single-sense appeal word) as the Bible does. There are full stories
(so-called illustrations and parables), abbreviated stories (exam-

4. Proverbs 26:9 (Berkeley).

ples), and mini-stories (instances; not really stories but the kernels of stories).

Young and old alike respond favorably to good stories. Stories strongly appeal to the senses; they provide room for multiple-sense appeal. One reason why the common people "gladly" heard Christ was that He used so many stories; stories bridge the gap between the intellectual and the common man.

Jesus used all three sorts of stories mentioned above. He told parables, gave examples (cf. the examples of the Galileans who were slaughtered and the eighteen on whom the tower in Siloam fell [Luke 13:1-5] and the example of Zacharias, the son of Barachias, "whom you murdered between the temple and the altar" [Matt. 23:35]), and he used instances ("Look at the birds of the sky," "Consider the lilies of the field" [Matt. 6:26, 28]).

Some stories, like parables, are true stories; others are more story-like (the listener, who knew about the Galileans, the eighteen, and Zacharias, knew the story already and was expected to fill it in). References to the birds and lilies are not really stories. They are more like suggestions of stories, more like snapshots instead of movies. However, these cameo shots are highly evocative. We shall focus on the true story.

The mistake that some preachers make when they discover the evocative power of a story is to tell stories and do little else. Their sermons become a string of pearls, in which a string of stories are suspended on a theme. Now each of these stories may be a natural pearl, but Christ sent us to preach His Word, not to string necklaces.

When a listener leaves church, there are four things he should take away, and stories should be a means to that end:

1. A clear understanding of the meaning and *telos* of the preaching portion,
2. A knowledge of how God wants him to change,
3. An understanding of what he must do to effect the change, and how, and

4. An assurance that all the preacher said came from the Scriptures and therefore is authoritative.

Telling stories, if that is all a preacher does, fails to accomplish these things.

If stories are told, they must be told well. Few things are as disappointing as leading the congregation to think it is in for a treat by announcing a story and then botching it for them by ineptness. Stories should be rehearsed until you are convinced you can tell them effectively. If the climax depends on a punch line, write it into your outline so you can refer to it if you fear you will forget it.

The best stories, like most of Christ's parables, have to do with persons in action and/or conversation. Dialogue enhances any story. You can see how much dialogue Jesus used by consulting a modern translation of the parables in which dialogue appears within quotation marks. Consider Christ's extensive and powerful use of dialogue in Luke 15:11-32. Indeed, at one point (vv. 18, 19), as the son rehearses what he will say to his father, there are quotes within quotes. And that, notice, is in a passage where there is only one person present—a place where most preachers would never think to use dialogue. But God is fond of this approach; that is why in Psalm 14:1 the fool says within his heart, ''There is no God.''

Dialogue appeals to the senses. You can ''hear'' the son as he speaks to himself in Christ's parable. Dialogue brings the listener into the story as an eavesdropper, and virtually turns it into a here-and-now event. Learn to use dialogue, then; freckle your stories with quotation marks.

Notice too that while adjectives are used (''*wild* living,'' ''*bad* famine''), the appeal is made largely through the impact of the story itself; adjectives help the story along; they are *not* used by the narrator as a substitute for good story telling (''Now, I want you to hear a *great* story''). Don't tell the listener the story is great, sad, etc.; let him draw his own conclusions. Stories, told well, need no such prefatory assistance. Weak preachers, instead, rely on adjectives rather than the story for effect and rarely achieve the effect wanted.

What is the shape or format of the story? In the following diagram you will find all the basic elements of a good story. Note well, this paradigm is basic; there are variations on the theme.

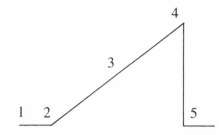

In this diagram there are

1. background (briefly sketched; e.g., Luke 15:11, 12),
2. a complication or problem (Luke 15:13),
3. suspense (Luke 15:14-21),
4. climax (Luke 15:22, 23), and
5. conclusion (Luke 15:24).

In Luke 15 there is an added story appended (vv. 25-32). Because this story itself is the epilogue and major climax of the three preceding parables, it is a special instance. Its impact depends on the background in Luke 15:1, 2 and the *contrast* of the epilogue with the three parables. From this, then, you can see immediately something of the wide possibilities for variety.

Look back again at the diagram. It serves three functions. The diagram indicates:

a. the order of events in the story,
b. the length of time devoted to each, and
c. the level of listener interest at each point (interest should peak at the climax).

Background material begins on a normal, acceptable level of interest. The introduction of a *complication* raises this level of tension, and additional complications added to that create a higher and ever-growing level of *suspense*. Then at the peak of emotion is the *climax*. Quickly emotion, interest, and tension drop. That is why the *conclusion* must be brief, made in a forceful line or two; often the climax itself is all that is needed (remember how annoying it is to have someone explain the punch line of a joke when you got it!). But notice that the twist Christ put on the third parable, when He added the epilogue about the elder brother, once again added complication and built suspense to a climax and conclusion far more powerfully than might have been expected.

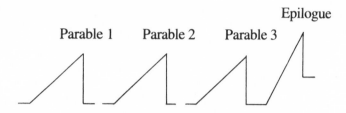

Use stories, then, but use them purposefully.

"What are the purposes of stories?" you ask. Here are seven:

1. to clarify truth,
2. to concretize and personalize truth, integrating principles with life today,
3. to make truth memorable,
4. to demonstrate how a principle works,
5. to back a claim,
6. to create interest, and
7. to involve the listener.

All of these uses of the story are self-evident and do not need examples (abbreviated stories) to clarify them.

Whenever you are tempted to use a story, be sure that it serves a purpose (don't tell it merely "because it's about time for another story" or *merely* for interest value), and be sure that you know exactly what purpose (or purposes) it serves. Frequent reference to this list (or a photocopy of it) while working on sermons will help you develop a sense of when a story is appropriate.

"How do I learn how to tell a story?"

Practice. But practice *outside* the pulpit; and do it *every* day. As you drive home in the evening, instead of becoming aggravated with the traffic, rehearse a story about something that happened to tell your wife and family when you arrive. They will love it, and, as your story-telling powers increase and bleed over into your sermons, your congregations will love it too. In this practice context you can also freely experiment with sounds, gestures, and other bodily expressions of meaning to your heart's content. All of this practice, if persisted in daily, in time (six months?) should have an appreciable effect on your preaching. All of which leads to a brief discussion of sound and of bodily action in relation to sense appeal.

Sound

Even though the principal medium with which preachers work is the medium of sound, they rarely use sound in evoking sense stimulation. There is a great, untapped resource here. The Greek sound *ouai*, translated "woe" in the New Testament (cf. Matt. 23), is more of an exclamation or groan of pain, displeasure, or anger than an actual word. This sound is interjected much the same way we use sounds like "ouch!" or "ahhh!" or "oh!" Jesus didn't hesitate to utter such sounds; neither should we! Onomatopoetic words ("buzz," "bang," etc.) are sounds that have turned respectable by becoming words. Stiff professionalists rarely even use them, let alone mere groans and other sounds! Yet, these often have great appeal to the senses. Learn to use words and sounds appropriately and forcefully. The freest preachers know how to use them and do not hesitate in doing so. Listen to a good storyteller and you will hear him making all sorts of noises. Sprinkle these freely into the mix of your daily practice sessions and notice how they improve the flavor.

I shall have more to say about the use of voice and body later on. But for now, here is a concluding note on the use of the body in relationship to sense appeal.

Bodily Action

The preacher works not only in the medium of sound but also in the medium of sight. Modern TV lingo has helped us to think of the members of our congregations not only as *listeners* but also as *viewers*. Preachers, take this to heart: you are being *watched,* not merely heard.

A powerful way to appeal to the senses is through bodily action. Surely, gestures, facial expressions (especially in smaller congregations), bodily movement, etc., all play an important part. In description, for instance, to say, and at the same time show by means of the hand, "I was this high," is usually effective, often much more effective than to attempt to describe height by words alone. Gestures are also used to indicate ("that one over there") and for emphasis: "No!" as the fist strikes the podium is more emphatic than the word alone.

Much more could be said about the interplay of these four factors in sense appeal, but for now what I have said should help you to make a good beginning.

Class Assignments:

1. Study five other parables of Christ and report on your findings.
2. Write a paper on the use of evocative language in five proverbs, each of which appeals to a different one of the five senses. Explain exactly what is done and how the appeal is made.

15

GATHERING
STORYTELLING MATERIALS

"But where do I go to get materials for stories? How do I think up examples and instances?" These questions are important enough to consider at some length.

In one way or another, the whole world is analogous to biblical truth. Because the world is God's world, His general revelation of Himself and His ways, whatever is in it will harmonize with His special revelation, the Bible. This is true because God is the Author of both, and He never contradicts Himself. So you don't have to look very far for your material. Wherever you are at the moment, look around you. All the material you need for the next 10 years could be found by sitting right there—in your study, or wherever you are—if you will only fully open all your senses to it and set your mind to work on chiseling what you find there into usable shapes.

"Ten years' worth of illustrations in my study? I suppose you mean in my books?"

No, without opening a single book—though there is certainly much there too.

"Well, now, preaching twice a week, a couple of weeks off for vacation, that means I preach roughly a hundred sermons a year. If I preach for 10 years, that would be a thousand sermons. And if I used an average of five illustrations per sermon, that would amount to five thousand illustrations! That many illustrations in *my study?* You must be kidding.''

No, I'm not; they are all there. In fact, you could preach from the material in your study for the rest of your life and not exhaust it. Now, I wouldn't advise you to restrict yourself to gathering all your future material from your study, or even the next 10 years' worth because, unless you were very careful, you'd find yourself falling into too much sameness. But a preacher who has learned the secret could do it without sameness, standing on his head (which, by the way, would give you a brand new vantage point)! However, I do suggest most strongly that you confine yourself to finding four out of the five stories you mentioned in your study for the next six months, and that you take the fifth from incidents, conversations, and events that involve people in action. The four out of five ''illustrations'' (as you called them) for the most part will likely have to do with simple comparisons and contrasts, relating more to things and their functions. This is the easiest way to begin. It will *force* you to open up your senses to *all* that is around you.

Here is how I suggest that you go about doing it:

1. *Every* day, after prayer, in a notebook purchased for that purpose (or on a 3 x 5 note card if you follow my shirt-pocket filing system[1]), write out two stories, examples, etc., suggested by something in your study.
2. *Don't* do anything else until you have them written out (don't be concerned about how good they are).
3. If more than two occur, write them all down.
4. On Saturday, go over them and put them in good form and language. File them topically (give each a topic heading) or textually. If you don't know which way is better, file topically and cross-reference textually. Throw out any real bummers, but keep even those that show but slight promise (on another day they might prove more fruitful).

After doing this regularly for four or five months, you should find

---

1. For more on this, see my *Shepherding God's Flock.*

material coming your way in profusion, and the likelihood is that, on the whole, its quality will continue to improve.

Now, for the next six months, write up at least two "illustrations" each day from what you find in the church auditorium. When you begin to do this, you will find that in preaching you will be able to say, "Now, take the sound of that radiator over there, . . ." or "Doubtless you have noticed that the aisles of this church are carpeted in red. Did you ever consider . . . ," etc. People will soon wonder if you are pulling them out of the air on the spot. When you are able to preach from your surroundings, as Jesus did when He spoke of the birds flying in the sky and when He said, probably with a sweep of the hand, "Consider the lilies," you will begin to understand something of the power and effectiveness of this form of "illustration."

"Well, I can see that it would be effective to do that, but just how do I develop my senses to the point where I can see and hear such things?"

By structure and practice. The structure I refer to is the six-months limitation to the study, and then to the church auditorium. Practice, practice, practice! If you patiently do so, good material in plentiful supply will begin to flow your way.

Let's see how it works. Right now, stop. Be silent, very silent. What do you hear? Make an effort to hear those sounds that you have learned to mask and ignore. Yes, there is the tick of a clock. Did someone on the other side of the building slam a door? (That doesn't count; it wasn't a sound originating in the study; neither is the sound of that bird call outside the window.) Ah, there's one—the squeak of your swivel chair. "Needs oiling," you say to yourself. Good. What else around here needs oiling? The official board? The church as a whole? The church communication system (and I don't mean the grapevine)? How about your prayer life? Will you be preaching to a congregation of squeaky, rusty Christians this Sunday?

Keep on listening. "Hey! Listen to my felt tip pen scratching on the margin of this book as I make a note." Good, you're beginning to hear again. Think for a moment; what could that sound represent? The rapidity or slow deliberateness with which life is spelled out? No, that's not so good—you think about it and see what you can come up with.[2]

Now, let's touch some things. Rub your hand on the window pane. Cold? Is there something in that? Sure, but it may not occur to you at once.[3] Stay with it—say, there you are: my greasy fingers smudged the window and left a mark. And they didn't even seem greasy to me! Hmmmm . . . I've got it: that is the average Joe who smears life up by sinful ways he doesn't even recognize. He can see them only when He looks at life through God's window pane, the Bible. That's got promise; but it'll need plenty of shaping up on Saturday.

Now, run your fingers over the concrete block wall. Rough? Right. But also solid, sturdy, and tough. Like what? I don't know. What do you think?

Next, try smelling.

"Smelling?"

Smelling. You may look foolish as you go around smelling things all over your study, but go ahead anyway; there isn't anyone looking. Smell the ink of a freshly printed book. It is as pleasant, unpleasant as a _____ (you fill in the blank). Smell the odor of heated dust on your lamp's glowing light bulb. Smell your hands; some faint trace of breakfast there? Or the slight aroma of the soap with which you washed them? What do you smell? And, what is it like?

Once again, start tasting. Taste a finger. Salty? Taste a piece of paper or chalk; flat? Taste some dust from the aspirins in that bottle in your desk; bitter? Something there about bitter pills? Perhaps.

And, of course, look. I saved this till the last, since this is most likely what you would have started with. But that is so easy, and there is so much to see, you might never have gotten to the other four

---

2. Here I am freely writing whatever comes into my head without modification. This is rough material; yours will be too. Don't get discouraged with it. On Saturday you can sort through it, find the best material, and shape it up.

3. When you have a few sermon ideas to "illustrate" at the beginning of your search, it is easier to know how to use what you find.

senses. Look around you, not just at objects, but at their parts. See what I mean?

When you begin to search for materials found among people around you who are doing and saying things, you may wish to carry 3 x 5 cards on which to jot down notes. Don't search for only what is unusual or sensational. Settle for the common and ordinary. See, hear, smell, etc., in the ordinary circumstance *more* than you ever have before, just as you have been learning to do in your study.

What can you discover in that tired, worn mother over there trying to still her crying baby? It thinks only of itself; she thinks only of it. How like Christ's love. How about that battered up old truck rumbling down the street? My, what stories those dents could tell! Why not imagine what some of them are? Listen to that man cough as he lights up his cigarette and takes the first puff; something's there, isn't it? Open your senses, open them widely to the world around you. Breathe it in with every breath, then put your mind in gear and think about what you have taken in.

Saturday, remember, is revision day. Take an hour and go over what you have done. You'll want to junk some (less and less as time goes on) and completely rewrite others. In the rewriting, two things will happen:

1. You will want to put your material into better form (work especially on arrangement and language).
2. You will want to make some entirely new uses, or applications, of some of your material. New analogies may occur.

You may not like to do this sort of work. You may think that the great preachers never had to do any of it. You are wrong. They did. Each, in his own way, worked tirelessly to discipline his senses and his mind to produce. When such a preacher now seems to shake dozens of stories and examples out of his sleeve like a magician, remember, there was a time when he found it every bit as difficult as you do to produce "illustrations." If you want to be able to do what he does some day, then right now you must also do what he did yesterday: practice, practice, practice. Good preaching, like anything else good, is hard work. But there are few things more rewarding than learning how to preach well.

"What about materials in books, magazines, and newspapers? Should I use these?"

Sure, so long as you make your own use of them. And be sure to use all sources fairly: cite references, give credit. But avoid books of illustrations and examples and stories in other men's sermons. Using these will make you lazy and dependent; you will never develop your own power of illustrating. Find your own material. What is truly yours will sound like it; much of what isn't will sound like it too! Other preachers' materials also will often be stale.

Now, let me mention what I have called the *jelling factor*. In time, you will discover that you have developed a certain ability to manufacture story material on the spot, while preaching. In *Pulpit Speech* I described the phenomenon this way:

> There is also the possibility in extemporaneous speaking for the use of on-the-spot insights, or for the operation of what I prefer to call the *jelling factor*. Every good extemporaneous preacher, after preaching, has written into his outline thoughts which occurred to him while he was preaching and which he used on the spot. They just seemed to jell in a way in which they would not jell in the study. Jelling, I must hasten to say, is the *result* of good preparation, and not a replacement for it. The jelling factor is the fruit or culmination of careful preparation and long thought prior to the delivery of the sermon. During the full concentration due to the tension of the preaching experience, at the moment of delivery certain ideas jell. Jelling gives a spontaneity and sparkle to speaking that the calm composition of full manuscripts done solely in the study is unable to bring to it. This is understandable since there is a comparative quiet and lack of tension in the study, where full manuscripts are prepared.[4]

Let me add just one note on the jelling factor. Don't fall into the temptation to use jelling materials when you first begin to discover them coming. If you do, you will be using only half-jelled substance; the idea may be good, but it won't hold together because the form will not be. Take it home and work with it until you have perfected it for

4. P. 114.

future use. It will keep if you put it on ice. Little by little, as you patiently work at preaching in the right ways, material will more and more often appear fully jelled and immediately useful. But it will be quite some time, and it will take a lot of preaching before that happens.

The wide-awake preacher is gathering material all the time, wherever he is, whether he sets out to look for it or not. Once he opens his senses to what is going on around him, he will see, hear, smell, etc., more and more. Material will soon come to him, and he will not have to search for it. In time he will develop a "set" toward all of life that will let little that is worthwhile get through his net.

Now, one last comment. Many preachers use Scripture, especially the Old Testament, illustratively. Don't do it. Always use the Bible authoritatively; never illustratively. Scripture was not given merely to illustrate points; it was written to make points. If you don't pay attention to this warning, the first thing you know, you will find yourself making points *you* want to make and using (misusing) the Bible to illustrate and back up *your* ideas. Psychologizers do this all the time.

This is a subtle temptation because those who use the Bible illustratively think that, by doing so, they will become more biblical than those who, with Christ, talk about birds and flowers. Nowhere do New Testament preachers use the Old Testament illustratively; whenever the Bible is quoted, it is quoted as God's authoritative Word on the point at issue.

So, work; work hard on gathering materials and you (and your congregation) will be delighted with the results.

Class Assignments:

1. Begin gathering material from your study. Work these over on Saturday and present the first week's crop in the form of a written report.
2. In the report, also include one fully written example garnered from classroom activity during the week to come.

16

A PREACHING STYLE

Style is language usage. Everyone has a style the moment he speaks, whether he is aware of the fact or not. The issue, therefore, is not whether you will have a style; you do—that can't be avoided—the only question is whether your style is good or bad. The question to ask is whether your style obscures, warps, or otherwise distorts God's truth, or whether it wings it home to hearts with power and effectiveness. Style helps or hinders; it is never neutral. Which does your style do? Does truth have a hard time flowing through you because of a constrictive style? If so, that is a matter of first importance for you to attend to.

The purpose of style is to provide an appropriate and effective medium for communicating content. I have already written about the use of evocative words, the sub-purpose of which is to help listeners enter into, and more fully experience, truth. That was a specific matter of style. Now we must discuss style more generally.

What makes one preacher's language dull, ineffective, and obscure while another's is gripping, powerful, and limpid? Two distinct styles. One has a good preaching style while the other does not. The first question we must tackle, then, is what is a good preaching style?

Many preachers seem to think a preaching style is a thing apart—a style that has little or no relationship to anything else in the known world. Or, at least that's what one is tempted to conclude when he listens to them. This stilted, so-called "preacher's style" is pock-marked with King James's terminology and Elizabethan or pseudo-Elizabethan constructions like, "beloved," "unto," "like unto," "sepulchre" (often mispronounced "sepluchre"), "beseech," "the person of," (as in "trust in the person of Christ" when "trust Christ" would do), "babe," "vale," "blessed," etc.

"Surely, this all-too-typical style isn't what you are asking me to develop, is it?"

Absolutely not. It is that sort of thing—unknown to the apostles, who spoke an elevated fish-market Greek,[1] and to the translators of the Authorized Version who wrote exactly as they talked. This style, one that has turned off so many young people, is a modern travesty totally without previous history or biblical warrant or example. You must thoroughly launder your style of all such "preachy" language.

Nor am I advocating the scholastic, technical, super-sophisticated bookish styles that other preachers develop. When they preach, they sound like the latest theological treatise.[2] Technical language has its place, but not in the pulpit. The great biblical, theological terms must be used, but not without explanation, nor should they be used in profusion.

And if, on the other hand, you think I am promoting the sort of chatty, so-called "conversational style" that majors on using the latest slang and jargon of the day and that lacks all form or order, then you are wrong about that too.

A good preaching style is a plain (but not drab), unaffected (but not unstudied) style that gets in there and gets the job done without calling attention to itself. It is clear and appropriate at every point to the message. Content should control this style. When content is relaxed, the style should relax; when it is tense, style must reflect that too.

1. Elevated by the message they preached.
2. For more on the use of technical and theological language, see my *Pulpit Speech*, pp. 47, 48.

Style is content's right-hand man, ready to run any errand that content requests of him. He will not dawdle along the roadside, playing with flowers. Nor will he run ahead of his leader when strolling along together. Indeed, his task is to anticipate and assist content's every intent. The more they work together, the more readily they begin to approximate one another.

This good preaching style measures up to the good, standard, accepted speech of the day. Newscasters on TV probably come as close to setting such a standard for us as anyone. The preacher's style will be a cut or two above the standard because of the greatness of the themes with which he deals. But he will never allow his style to remain, as many—perhaps most—preachers do, at a level lower than that used on TV.

Language usage is a complex matter. All of us learn our basic speech and language habits early in our homes, long *before* we can read; the spoken word comes first. And therefore we learn by imitation. That is why most Southerners pronounce "pin" and "pen" identically, why some Easterners say "Africar," and why the rest of us do not. As we progress in our ability to understand language and communicate through speech, our teachers and peers also become speech models for us. The average 21-year-old adult is a product that is a conglomerate of the various speech models after which he unconsciously patterned his speech.

Modeling has to do not only with pronunciation and regional melody patterns,[3] but also to a greater extent with word choice, expressions, and grammar. "I'm fixin' to do it," would not be heard in most parts of the U.S., but it is standard fare for both cultivated and uncultivated Southerners, just as "you 'uns" is accepted by most in some parts of western Pennsylvania.

"Well, if I'm largely a product of my past, I guess I'm just stuck with my style. Right?"

Wrong.

Because speech is a learned activity, it is relearnable. Although

3. Such as rising to a higher pitch at the end of a sentence even when not asking a question.

physiology may develop along with certain speech sounds, making it more difficult later in life to learn others, that problem almost exclusively has to do with learning a second language and, of course, has nothing whatever to do with working vocabulary expansion and grammatical structures.

It is certainly an advantage to grow up in a home in which nearly perfect grammar is used, in which its members daily put large, working vocabularies to use, and in which they express themselves precisely, clearly, and interestingly. It is difficult to find out later on in life that one's speech legacy is inaccurate, pedestrian, and imprecise. Such a style will ill-fit the proclamation of God's holy Word and must be changed. The person with good speech models from the outset has a distinct advantage over others, while the one who has grown up with poor models is, at first, greatly disadvantaged. And often that is how it continues through life. But, if he only will, the speech disadvantaged person can turn his disadvantage into an asset. The first man's background serves him more than adequately, so he may see no need to study, develop, and grow in his speaking skills. But in dozens of ways the second man comes hard up against the fact that his grammar and working vocabulary are substandard. If he will only take this problem to heart and do all he can to work to improve his speech, in the end he may find himself out in front of his more advantaged friend. Surely fishermen, such as some of the apostles were, must have spent time working on their speech, to be able to speak and write as effectively as they did.

Modifying inadequate speech habits is a long, tedious task, but it is rewarding and well worth the time and effort that must be devoted to it. I know; I have had to do it. It has taken me years. Indeed, I have not yet stopped working at it; every year I work through a couple of books on grammar, style, or some other aspect of language.

"What must I do to make the necessary changes, and how do I begin?"

Let me offer some practical suggestions. First, visit your local college or university speech and English departments. Explain your problem and ask if they offer any diagnostic courses, designed to help you discover your deficiencies. Your first problem will be to become aware of and to precisely identify every weakness that must be eliminated. What you are looking for is a course that will help you to discover poor grammar and poor word usage. Don't waste time taking other sorts of courses. If there is no such course available, you will have to develop your own. The advantage of a course is that you will have (1) expert help and (2) disciplined structure.

Because it takes about six weeks of daily effort to make a habit change (change is a two-factored process where you put off and put on[4]), most preachers don't persist; they are impatient and give up too soon. You must determine to persevere. If you truly want to honor Christ and avoid any distortion of His truth arising from faulty communication patterns, you will be adequately motivated to persist until you get results. The first three-week period is a time of awareness, of learning new ways, of self-conscious and awkward attempts at change; the second three-week period is a time of becoming accustomed to the new pattern, of developing skill and precision in its use, and beginning to feel comfortable with it. By the end of the six-week period, the new pattern should have become automatic and unconscious.

Now, put together these two thoughts:

1. I must learn what my deficiencies are;
2. I must replace each deficiency with its proper alternative by daily work over a six-week period.

That is the outline for your basic program, however you may care to orchestrate it.

But what else do those two thoughts imply? If you have a large number of deficiencies, it is going to take quite a while and a lot of patience, not to speak of the necessary effort you must expend, to overcome them. But, if you approach the problem properly, that conclusion should not deter you. Stop looking at the forest; start working on a few trees. Many forests have been leveled with axes, but none all at once.

---

4. Cf. *The Christian Counselor's Manual* on the put off/put on dynamic.

Now let's move ahead. Diagnosis. If you can't obtain help at a local university speech department, then let's see what you can do on your own. Here is one way to proceed.

1. Write down every *known* deficiency in vocabulary usage and in grammar. You are probably aware of some already. Ask you wife and a couple of close friends to make a few suggestions.
2. Then, using a tape recorder,
   a. record about five sermons (or better still, if you have some already, use these),
   b. and about the same number of casual conversations in normal, unrehearsed contexts (possibly different problems will emerge in unprepared contexts).
   c. Together with one or two friendly persons who can help, listen to these tapes and isolate substandard practices in vocabulary usage and in grammar (be careful not to play back any conversations that anyone else should not be allowed to hear).
   d. Add these substandardisms to your original list.
3. Determine which four (two vocabulary problems and two grammatical) problems you think might be the most serious or most obvious and troublesome to others. Look especially for glaring grammatical blunders such as, "He don't live there," and "He don't have none," as well as vocabulary limitations, vagaries ("thing," "stuff"), or over-uses (along with these, note all appendages such as "you know?" or "O.K.?") that you may have gotten into the habit of affixing to sentences).

The wrong use of "don't" for "doesn't," mentioned above, stands out vividly to those who know better, as does the double negative, "don't . . . none," and impossible combinations like "most unique." These, therefore, would be good grammatical usages to target for change over the next six weeks. Not only do these incorrect forms protrude, but because they are commonly used constructions they *constantly* call attention to themselves.

The habit of using vague terms such as "thing" or "stuff" ("Then he had another thing with which he . . . ," "There was lots of stuff like that"), instead of the word or words that more precisely describe the object or action about which one wishes to communicate, is a bit more difficult to work with. Your friends can help some in picking out various other flaws, but you yourself will have to learn to be vicious with your own sermons or you will not pick up all your flaws. Some men become so enamored with their own voices on tape that they can hear nothing amiss. Learn instead to be heavily self-critical.

Try to discover if you tend to become vague only in certain areas of thought, or whether the habit persists generally. If you can isolate and identify a particular area, then you can work especially to avoid problems when approaching it in the future. Many preachers, for instance, don't take time to look up specific words that pertain to an area of life with which they have little familiarity; so they become vague when mentioning anything having to do with agriculture, business, or whatever it may be. Simply looking up key words, together with their meanings and usages, can be a great help.

What you should be looking for at the end of all this effort is *full fluency*. That is your goal and the purpose for modifying your present speech habits. Fully fluent speech calls no attention to itself while effectively communicating content to the listener. It enables the congregation to focus attention on the message rather than on the messenger. Fluent speech enables the preacher to get out of the way of the truth; that is the concern we have.

A good preaching style, then, is one that serves content well. Good style doesn't call attention to itself because of its idiosyncrasies or its deficiencies. It moves smoothly ahead, surefootedly making tracks toward its destination without taking the listener down any by-ways and without stumbling.

Style is a *means* of bringing a message to the listener; it must never become an end in itself. At every point, therefore, style should parallel content, sensitively adjusting not only to the more overt changes in the content itself, but also to the more subtle nuances of its modifications in tone and mood.

But just what is this "full fluency" of which I have been speaking? Full fluency is the ability to pick the right words (those that are oral, precise, evocative, and appropriate) at high speed, and the ability to combine them into easily understood, gripping speech.

Full fluency requires proper vocabulary usage. Most attempts to solve problems of poor word usage offer little help for the preacher. These all suggest the building of larger vocabularies ("It pays to increase your word power"). Of course, regular habits of vocabulary building should continue all through life.[5] But, as important as that is, it will never solve the preacher's problem. The average college student has a recognition vocabulary of over 250,000 words; seminary graduates far excel that number. Yet Shakespeare used only 25,000 words—but what words! What word *usage!* It is not a larger vocabulary that you need.

What you lack is not a recognition vocabulary; it is a vital, everyday, working vocabulary that you lack. You need to learn to *use* more of the vocabulary that you already have—and to use it more effectively. Some preachers buy books to put on their shelves; others to use. Words in a recognition vocabulary, like the books on the shelves, will do little good until they are used. Accumulation of more and more books and words is not the answer.

As lazy sinners, we tend to rely on too few words to accomplish our tasks. We also fall into the sluggardly habit of using cliches and trite phrases (if anything fails to communicate, it is this). We so overwork these words, along with our long-suffering congregations, that they both become weary and sluggish. By failing to recognize that there is a best word or phrase to express every thought, we settle for mediocre and second-rate ways of saying things. We have not taken the time to search for the best.

Well, what can be done? Here are four steps you can take to put to better use the vocabulary you already possess:

1. *Be concrete.* Avoid abstractions wherever you can. Don't say "car." Rather, tell us it was a 1981 bronze-colored Toyota Tercel with orange stripes running along the sides. Abstractions force the listener to fill in too much material on his own.

---

5. These are: (1) regular use of the dictionary: look up the meaning of *every* word you encounter that you do not know *precisely;* (2) learning the proper pronunciation of each word; (3) using these words, if appropriate, in everyday conversation; (4) learning precise connotations as well as denotations of each term.

But many listeners won't—and go to sleep. They are too lazy, lack imagination to do so, etc. Others, valiantly trying to stay with you in spite of everything, may fill in all sorts of wrong content that distorts your message and leads to misunderstanding.

2. *Be precise.* Choose the *exact* term; do not settle for those living somewhere in its vicinity. To be in the right neighborhood is not enough; you must get the address and find the very house where your word or phrase lives.

3. *Be ruthless.* Cut from your speech all trite expressions, cliches, vague terms, meaningless repetitions, long, complex sentences, abstractions, and jargon. In each case locate, instead, an acceptable alternative and use it until it replaces the offending item. Again, develop self-critical habits. Become your own severest critic. But be sure your criticism always, in each instance, results in better practice; there is little value in the sort of self-criticism that merely discourages but never leads to improvement.

4. *Be persistent.* Practice. Practice until you have mastered whatever you are seeking to learn. Practice until you have replaced all poor patterns with good ones. Stick closely to the six-week, daily practice routine I have explained. Practice using more and more of the rich vocabulary you already possess—until it begins to possess you. Practice in casual situations daily. DO NOT WORK ON LEARNING NEW WORDS. DO NOT PRACTICE WHILE PREACHING. Soon you will preach what you practice. In time, the vocabulary you have introduced into informal situations will find its way over into more formal ways, all by itself, with little or no conscious help from you.

But this is work, hard work. There is no easy way to make the change. Remember why you are going to go to all this effort: it is because you want to develop a style that, rather than calling attention to itself, will be so clear, so appropriate, and so accurate that, without distortion, it will convey God's truth with power to needy listeners. Any preacher who does not find that a compelling purpose to pursue ought either to repent or reexamine his call to the ministry.

Do not misunderstand the intent of this chapter. I have no desire to turn you into an orator. I don't want you to become a preaching

Demosthenes. What I am concerned about is a style that will call no attention to itself. The orator calls attention to himself: people go away saying, "What a wonderful speech!" But the preacher with an abominable style also calls attention to himself. People say, "What a terrible sermon!" When they walk away from our sermons, we want them to say neither; let them say only one thing: "What a wonderful Christ!"

Class Assignment:

Take time to make a list of your stylistic deficiencies as you know them. Be ready to share these in class in a discussion on how best to begin to deal with these problems in the context of this course.

17

COUNSELING
AND PREACHING

I have said something already about the relationship of preaching to counseling. In that place I noted how the regular study of the Scriptures required for any biblical ministry—including counseling ministry—is enhanced by the weekly discipline of exposition and application that is required by preaching. And I observed also that, on the other hand, preaching that has been forged not only in the study but in the counseling room as well tends to be quite different from, and more personal than, preaching that is not. I also implied that a positive response is more likely to be elicited by such personalized preaching than from preaching that knows nothing of the effective use of the preaching portion in counseling. All of this, and much more, is true because God Himself joined preaching and counseling together as two sides of one ministry of His Word.[1] What God has joined together let no man put asunder.[2]

1. ". . . that I didn't hold back in declaring anything that was beneficial to you and in teaching you publicly and from house to house" (Acts 20:20). ". . . Whom we announce, counseling every person and teaching every person as wisely as possible, so that we may present every person mature in Christ" (Col. 1:28).
2. Historically, the divorce between preaching and counseling took place when

Because preaching and counseling are thus interrelated, not only the content, but the principles and practices common to both when interfaced, inform and strengthen each other. In this chapter, therefore, I shall suggest to you several ways in which an understanding of biblical counseling may be of assistance in your preaching. I must presuppose you are at least familiar with the roots and basic tenets of nouthetic counseling; there is no possibility of establishing these here. If you are not, I must refer you to any or all of my following titles: *Competent to Counsel, The Christian Counselor's Manual, Lectures on Counseling, More than Redemption, Ready to Restore,* and *The Christian Counselor's Wordbook.* While these volumes by no means exhaust the available offerings, they will serve quite well to acquaint you with all you need to know to understand this chapter.

Problems

Counseling uncovers problems in persons that preachers must know about. These problems, unfortunately, do not appear only in the counseling room; they occur in the counselee's life at work, at home, at leisure, and at church. Because they do, they become barriers to preaching and its intended purposes, so it is not safe to ignore them when preaching.

But unless a preacher is alive to people and how they act, he will tend to neglect these problems, to the detriment of his preaching and the injury of his congregation. And, typically, because the existing homiletics textbooks, in a totally one-sided fashion, ignore the other half of the ministry of the Word, they offer virtually no help in analyzing, solving, or relating to preaching the many problems that await the unsuspecting preacher. Because he has been left vulnerable to them by naive writers and/or instructors who ought to know better, but don't, he unexpectedly runs up against problem after problem in preaching; it is

---

counseling came to be identified with psychotherapy rather than with the ministry of the Word. A return to a biblical stance on this matter makes the reunion of the two inevitable, thus bringing the possibility of new, helpful insights into preaching through an integration of principles and practices.

like someone trying to find his way across an unilluminated and totally unfamiliar terrain. It is no wonder, then, that so many preachers stumble around for years trying in vain to perfect their preaching. It is no wonder that they do not know what to do about the ineffectiveness of their public ministry and the minimal results they attain. Indeed, because they see so little change in the lives of their members, they sense that something is wrong, but they never suspect the trouble stems from a faulty understanding of those very members themselves. Instead, they go on buying homiletics textbooks, seeking earnestly to follow the advice they are given, but with little or no perceptible results. Of course, in following that procedure they do not find the help they seek—it simply isn't there. It is at long last time for a homiletics textbook to turn a floodlight of information toward the terrain on which they find themselves wandering and lost. Once the field has been properly lighted, and the location and nature of the many barriers and obstacles are apparent, something substantive can be done to improve on the current policies that amount to little more than thrashing about in the dark.

What are some of the barriers and obstacles to good communication that a preacher will discover when he examines the terrain? I shall note several (not all) suggestively:

1. *Excuse Making*

Excuses are hollow substitutes for reasons. Or, as Vance Havner once put it, "An excuse is the skin of a reason stuffed with a lie." Excuse-making is a way of avoiding responsibility, deflecting blame, and justifying sin. Counselors hear excuses every day: "Well, I would have done it, but you see. . . ." With many persons—very many— excusing one's self for one or more reasons has become a way of life. Unless you are aware of this tendency of sinful human beings and, at those places where they are likely to sidestep truth or injunction with an excuse, confront excuse makers with the impossibility of making any excuses that are acceptable to God, the impact of your message on them may be completely lost. When preaching, a counseling preacher will know at which points excuse makers tend to bail out of sermons and will be waiting for them at the door. He will not let them leave so easily. Moreover, he will be aware of the sorts of excuses that are likely to be made in response to the thrust of any given preaching portion, and will have a counter plan ready to meet them. For instance, at some point in his sermon such a preacher might be heard explaining,

Now, I know some of you might be saying to yourselves, "Well, that's fine for the young folk, but I'm too old to learn how to do that. You can't teach an old dog new tricks." Well, let me tell you, God didn't write these words to young people only. Remember what He said about change to Abraham as an old man, older than you? Excuse-making sears the conscience. That is a serious matter. By desensitizing God's early warning system, which is designed to make us feel bad when we disobey, at length you will eliminate a system that is one of your best friends. In the spiritual life, what you are thinking of doing is akin to destroying the pain-sensing nerve endings in your fingers. Without these you would not know to remove your hand from a hot stove until you began to smell meat burning. But that's too late. Don't let the excuse that it is too late to learn really make it too late for you. . . .

In Jesus' powerful sermon at Nazareth, at first "everybody spoke well about Him" and focused only on His manner of speaking: "They were surprised at what gracious words came from His mouth." They were ignoring His message. His preaching was eliciting no vital response. So Jesus, who knew what was happening, spoke directly to the problem:

And He said to them, "Doubtless you will quote this proverb: 'Physician, heal yourself; do here in your home town the same things that we have heard you did at Capernaum' " (Luke 4:23).

That statement anticipates the excuse that they would make: by the use of an old proverb that was designed to deflect responsibility from themselves back to Jesus, they would try to escape the thrust of what He was saying. But in these words and in those that follow, Jesus exposed their dodge and cut them off at the exit.

One of the most popular forms of excuse-making, a form that involves and alienates other people, is blame-shifting: "But, you see,

if my wife had only done her part, then I. . . ." Shades of the
Garden of Eden! How important it is also to expose and counter this
all-too-common form of excuse-making which is as old as the human
race. The biblical principle of sorting out responsibilities, which I
shall explain later on in this chapter, must be emphasized at those
points that call for joint, but individual, responsibilities.

2. Lack of Discipline

Many persons in your congregation lack discipline. That is to say,
they lack order, method, regularity, planning and scheduling ability,
perseverance, and/or commitment (all of which are vital ingredients
of discipline). A principal problem that stands in the way of edifying
members of the congregation, therefore, is their undisciplined ways
of attempting to appropriate the biblical truths and to carry out the
biblical injunctions about which you preach. As a result, thoughtful
counseling preachers know that it is essential to preach often about the
various aspects of discipline to which the Bible addresses itself
because they recognize that discipline is one of the roads their listeners must travel on the way to godliness:

> But avoid godless and old-womanish myths, and discipline your-
> self for godliness, . . . (I Tim. 4:7).

So, in preparing a given message, it will be well to ask yourself such
questions as

1. Will it require discipline for my congregation to do this?
2. Should I warn the congregation that this particular task can be
   accomplished only by a commitment to work at it prayerfully
   every day until it becomes habitual?
3. What aspects of discipline will my undisciplined members be
   most likely to stumble over, and how can I help them to avoid
   tripping and falling?

Preachers who don't ever grapple with such matters wonder why it
is only the faithful few (i.e., the *self-disciplined* few!) who latch onto
the truths that they preach, and why so many others (the *un*disciplined
crowd) fail to do so. One reason is that undisciplined persons, no

matter how noble their desires may be—and many such persons are deeply stirred by preaching and truly wish to respond rightly to it[3]—nevertheless fail in the doing because of their sloppy, sinful, undisciplined patterns and habits. To continue to bewail their failure, to flagellate yourself, or to give them a tongue lashing from the pulpit will not overcome the problem. Neither better exegesis nor more telling illustrations will help; these efforts, together with increased exhortation will lead only to increased frustration all around. The more you convict a person of the need to do something, and the more you build a desire in him to do it, the more you devastate him if he finds he is *unable* to do it. Undisciplined persons are *unable* to do many things until they repent and become disciplined. Yet they too may be unaware of the problem. It is possible that much of the seeming deadness and lethargy in your congregation stems directly from this problem or from one that is very similar to it (lack of ability to implement truth; see *infra*). The only way to solve the discipline problem is to clearly expose it and give instruction in biblical discipline. That instruction will mean more than merely *talking* about discipline; it will involve help in planning and scheduling, seeking commitments to specific programs and dates, and will require you to help them bring order out of the chaos in their spiritual lives.[4] Incidentally, it is not necessarily true that a person who knows how to discipline himself in his business or work will also know how to bring discipline to his spiritual life. But, if you see order and discipline in one or more areas of a person's life, you can show him (1) that he is capable of discipline, thus arousing hope, and (2) how he may apply many of the same principles and practices to biblical obedience.

While it is absolutely necessary for undisciplined persons to become disciplined, the problem is that they find it very difficult to do so without help because they are caught in the discipline dilemma: it takes discipline to become disciplined. That is why, in the Book of Proverbs, the need for outside help in bringing about discipline is so

---

3. If one has no such desire, his more basic problem may be laziness.
4. For further information on planning and scheduling, see *Shepherding God's Flock* in the appropriate places.

frequently emphasized. Discipline rarely comes easily. What is needed in most cases is heavy structure, with someone riding herd until the habitual side of the behavior begins to take form. Then the structure may be removed and supervision may be relaxed.

3. *Presence of Complicating Problems*

Like the lack of discipline, almost *any* other unsolved problem may interfere with one's desire or ability to respond to a given sermon as he ought, thus forming a barrier. When such a problem gets in the way, this sort of barrier is what I call a complicating problem. Complicating problems are not integrally related to the initial problem, but, nevertheless, in some way or another have intruded themselves into it and now block edificational progress. Therefore, complicating problems either must be dealt with first, before even beginning to attempt whatever it is that you are preaching about, or must be included as an aspect, or step in the process, of dealing with the initial problem that your sermon is designed to solve. If, for instance, you wish to speak about strengthening the husband/wife relationship through joint prayer, you will probably be wise to preach first about problems in relationships that destroy communication and joint effort of any sort in the home. Peter recognized the importance of the interrelatedness of such matters when he wrote:

> Husbands, likewise live with your wives in an understanding way, showing respect for the woman as you would for a fragile vase, and as joint heirs of the grace of life, so that your prayers may not be interrupted (I Pet. 3:7).

Peter made it perfectly clear that a bad relationship with one's wife leads to a bad relationship with God; communication problems on the horizontal level result also in problems of communicating with God.

Similarly, almost any other problem may get in the way of your achieving what you wish to bring about by your sermon. Therefore, unless you take such problems into account, you will end up spinning your sermon's wheels. And you will miss the very persons you want most to reach. Now, of course, you cannot anticipate all the complicating problems that might get in the way, nor could you refer to all the complicating problems that might exist in any congregational gathering on a given Sunday. But you can do two things:

1. Mention those that most likely may be tied to the subject, as Peter did;
2. Mention the issue itself from time to time, urging the members of the congregation themselves to discover, identify, and solve complicating problems or, in the event they do not know how to do so, to seek your help.

All of which leads us next to the greatest of all complicating problems:

4. *Failure to Repent*

Throughout this discussion, I am assuming that the persons to whom we refer are Christians with various problems. From I Corinthians 2:9-16,[5] Romans 8:8,[6] etc., it should be obvious that unbelievers will not and, indeed, cannot respond to edificational preaching in a satisfactory manner; it is foolish, therefore to attempt to edify them. They cannot be built up so long as they are unbelievers. You cannot build them up in the faith because they have no faith upon which to build. To build, there must first be a foundation, and that foundation must be Christ. The task with all such persons is to bring them to

---

5. "But as it is written: 'What the eye hasn't seen and the ear hasn't heard, and what hasn't been conceived by the human heart, is what God has prepared for those who love Him.' To us God revealed it by His Spirit. The Spirit searches into everything, even the deep thoughts of God. Who knows the thoughts of a person except the spirit of the person in him; so too no one knows God's thoughts except God's Spirit. Now we have not received the world's spirit but the Spirit Who is from God, so that we may know that which God has freely given to us. And it is these things about which we speak, not in words taught by human wisdom but in those that are taught by the Spirit, combining spiritual teaching with spiritual words. But a natural person doesn't welcome the teachings of God's Spirit; they are foolishness to him, and he isn't able to know about them because they must be investigated spiritually. But the spiritual person is able to investigate everything while (on the other hand) no one has the ability to investigate him. 'Who has known the Lord's mind; who will instruct Him?' But we have the mind of Christ" (I Cor. 2:9-16).

6. "And those who are in the flesh can't please God" (Rom. 8:8).

repentance toward God and faith toward our Lord Jesus Christ. Otherwise, your preaching becomes legalistic, attempting to get unbelievers to conform outwardly to God's commandment, in their own strength, apart from any inner change of heart.[7]

But the repentance about which I am speaking here is the repentance of sinning believers who, like David, are in misery because they have not yet confessed their sin and sought God's fatherly forgiveness (cf. Ps. 32:3, 4). Let me describe repentance to you in the words of *The Christian Counselor's Wordbook:*

> Repentance is an inner change of mind . . . toward one's self, toward God and toward others, that leads to an outer change of life. It may or may not result in restitution, as required, but, when genuine, always results in the desire and the attempt to abandon old sinful lifestyles and to adopt new, biblical ones. Repentance is a precondition to all biblical change that has to do with overcoming sin (some change in counseling is simply a matter of growth [p. 77]).

That repentance truly is "a precondition to all biblical change that has to do with overcoming sin" should be apparent immediately. Not only are "conviction" of sin and its "correction" (i.e., repentance) included as two of the steps of change listed in II Timothy 3:16, but the fact that repentance is necessary is clear on the face of it. How can you urge the establishment of new and better relationships between sinning parties who have been estranged from one another, for instance, without first calling on them to repent of their bitterness and resentment? Reconciliation, or any other "put on" must be preceded by the "put off" of that which it is designed to replace.[8] The beginning of the putting off of any sin is repentance. An unrepentant liar cannot become a truth teller; an unrepentant thief cannot become an honest, hard-working, sharing person; and the life of an unrepentant drunkard cannot be filled with the Spirit (cf. Eph. 4:25, 28; 5:18).

---

7. Heart in the Scriptures does *not* mean feelings or emotion, but the inner, hidden life known only to God and one's self. For a full discussion of heart, see my book, *More than Redemption.*

8. On the put on/put off dynamic, see *The Christian Counselor's Manual.*

Your preaching, therefore, must reflect this all-important fact that in such cases repentance must preclude progress.

I could continue to mention problem after problem that might become a barrier to successful preaching, but these are considered in depth in various places in my books on counseling. The four problems I have mentioned in this chapter, however, have been discussed not merely because of the frequency of their occurrence and the fact that the failure to bring them under consideration when preparing sermons accounts for so much of the failure in preaching, but also because I wanted to impress upon you the very great importance of taking such matters seriously when preparing and delivering sermons.

For further consideration, ask yourself, "How do I preach this message (i.e., whatever sermon you are now in the process of preparing) to persons who are full of self-pity, who are irresponsible, whose lives are dominated by ingrained habits that are antithetical to all I want to accomplish, who will be fearful about obeying, who are under a load of guilt, or who love the world too much? Furthermore, ask yourself, "How do I find out if such problems exist, and if so, which ones?" And furthermore, ask, "How would it be best to expose, counter, and overcome such barriers to edification?"

Obviously, if there are all sorts of problems, you can't tackle them all at once. So you must set up an order of priority based on (1) how seriously a given problem may affect congregational response, (2) how many persons are already involved in it, and (3) which barriers are basic to removing others. One person may be such a bad apple that he is likely to adversely affect the entire congregation with his attitude. In such cases in your preaching it may be essential to erect a preventive fence to ward off any attacks while dealing with him personally. There, it is the *seriousness* of the *threat* to the *whole* that raises matters of priority. Many similar considerations will be a matter of concern to the preacher-counselor who recognizes the great importance of such matters.

Principles

Not only may a preacher be informed by taking note of problems that arise in counseling and that become barriers to successful preaching, but he may find as well that a knowledge of counseling principles themselves will prove fruitful. By this, I do not mean that he will turn preaching into counseling from the pulpit, or that all the principles of counseling and preaching are interchangeable. If, however, he knows biblical counseling principles and keeps them in mind when preparing and delivering sermons, he will find them to be a great help. How is that so?

Again, rather than making an exhaustive or detailed study of counseling principles, I wish only to suggest a number of these. Others can be garnered from the basic counseling texts (but see especially *Ready to Restore*, pp. 32-38).

Take, for instance, the principle that change is a two-factored process. I have mentioned this already in my comments about putting on as well as putting off in my discussion of repentance. There I showed how it is wrong to preach putting on without, at the same time, preaching the need to put off. Even so, the opposite is just as true: when preaching about sinful patterns, it is wrong to think that lasting change can occur merely by preaching against something, by bringing someone to repentance, or by trying to *break* a habit. Putting off must be followed by putting on. Sinful patterns can be adequately changed only by *replacing* them with the biblical alternatives to them (cf. Eph. 4:22-24; Col. 3:5-14).

Earlier in this chapter I mentioned the importance of stressing the principle of sorting out responsibilities. People constantly must be shown that even when others have wronged them, that does not excuse them from assuming their responsibilities. In such situations there are always two responsibilities to be distinguished:

1. The responsibility of the one doing the wrong: he must be held responsible for his sin;
2. The responsibility of the one who is wronged: he must be held responsible to respond biblically to the wrong (cf. Rom. 12:14-21[9]).

9. For an exposition of this section, see my book, *How to Overcome Evil.*

It is common for a sinner to try to cover his wrongdoing by saying someone else "made me act as I did." But regardless of how one person mistreats another, he cannot *cause* sinful anger, ulcers, worry in the one who is mistreated. Jesus didn't get an ulcer on the cross; instead, He handled wrongdoing righteously. That is to say, when He prayed for those who were killing Him, He assumed His responsibility in the relationship. And, in every relationship, that is exactly what He calls on us to do. Therefore, in preaching, you must hold all parties to the responsibilities that, separately, devolve upon them. If you keep this principle in mind, you will neither speak carelessly about "cause,"[10] nor allow those who are wronged to slide off the hook about their responsibilities—as so many preachers do who, because they have done little biblical counseling, are unaware of the importance of these matters in people's lives. This is a key principle.

Remember, too, the importance of the listener's agenda. Be sure you make clear to the members of your congregation that when they do whatever it is you are asking them to do in your sermon, they must do it *to please God,* and *not as a gimmick* to get something they want. Thus, according to Ephesians 5:25, a husband should give himself to his wife (his time, his interest, his concern, his money and—if need be—his life). Fine; but he must not do it in order to bring himself peace, or to keep her from leaving him. He must do it *primarily* because God commands him to do so. That means he must continue to show love to his wife by giving himself to her whether this brings peace or not, whether she leaves him or stays. The person who does it *as a gimmick,* to get what he wants, will quit when he does not get what he wants. Pleasing God must have top priority. All other items on the counselee's agenda must take second place to it.

Any number of counseling principles, as I said, may be plugged into preaching; indeed, probably *most* biblically valid counseling principles relate to and are useful for preaching. Consider ten:

1. When seeking to bring about change, never attempt to do so

10. For proper language usage in this, and so many other areas, cf. my book, *The Language of Counseling.*

in the abstract; people change only in concrete ways. [11]

2. Always give hope. People will not persevere during the often difficult process of change without hope.

3. Never minimize the severity of problems; instead always maximize Christ and His power to solve problems.

4. If a person has a life-dominating problem, aim at total restructuring.

5. Always approach seemingly hopeless situations with emphatic disagreement. Empathy alone removes all possibility of help. Disagree when the counselee says "It's hopeless." Say, "It is difficult, but not too difficult for God."

6. Don't become oriented toward people's problems, but toward God's solutions.

7. Gauge how much change is now feasible; too little is boring, too much is discouraging.

8. Don't let people settle for less than the scriptural solution.

9. Use biblical, or biblically derived, language when analyzing and labeling problems, and when planning solutions to them.

10. Be commandment-oriented rather than feeling-oriented.

The list of counseling principles could be extended indefinitely, but surely, if you understand at all what I am getting at, you will grasp immediately the importance of using such principles as guides to the preaching of sermons. Now, finally, let us take a look at counseling.

Practices

Here, there will be less carry-over because practices conform more closely to the *medium* of ministry than do the problems encountered or the principles adopted. But there is one practice, so significant to both, that here I wish to discuss it alone, in depth: the use of *how to*. *How to,* or the implementation of biblical truth in actual day-by-day living, is just as important in preaching as it is in counseling.

In a later chapter, on implementation, I shall have more to say about this all-important matter, but for now I shall confine myself to a discussion of the Sermon on the Mount. Had homileticians adequately

---

11. For the rationale behind this, and the other nine principles, see my counseling books.

examined Christ's edificational preaching before, they might have saved pastors and their longsuffering congregations a considerable amount of unnecessary grief over the problem of implementation. Consider this:

1. The Sermon on the Mount is filled with *how-to* instruction; people are not left to flounder, knowing what they are supposed to do but not knowing how to do it. Every command is accompanied by *how to*.
2. The Sermon is filled also with how *not* to, warning against the perversions of God's commands that are so likely to occur among sinners.

Each of these elements in this sermon may be seen in the following chart:

IMPLEMENTATION
IN
THE SERMON ON THE MOUNT

Matthew 5:1-20: Introduction
Matthew 5:21–7:27:

Verses	Command	How not to obey it	How to obey it
Matt. 5:21-26	Don't murder.	Don't merely refrain from the act (21*b*,22).	Refrain from the attitude. as well as its outer expressions: a. wrong words (22). b. unreconciled condition (23, 24). c. court trials (25, 26).
vv. 27-31	Don't commit adultery.	Don't merely refrain from the act (27). Don't divorce for sinful reasons supposing that God's command in Deut. 24 refers only to having divorce proceedings in order.	Refrain from lustful desire and from looking lustfully at another (28). Create conditions that make it hard to sin (29, 30). Divorce only on grounds of fornication (32).

Verses	Command	How not to obey it	How to obey it
vv. 33-37	Don't swear.	Don't swear by: a. heaven (34). b. earth (35). c. Jerusalem (35). d. your head (36). Don't swear at all (33).	Let your yes mean yes, and your no mean no (37).
vv. 38-42	Do good to all men.	Don't use a civil law to justify personal revenge (38, 39).	Do good by: a. turning cheek (39). b. giving coat too (40). c. going second mile (41). d. giving and lending to those in need (42).
vv. 43-47	Love your enemies.	Don't love neighbors and hate enemies (43).	Love enemies by: a. praying for persecutors (44). b. being like Father, who does good to evildoers (45, 48).
Matt. 6:1-4	Give charity.	Don't give to be seen by others: a. don't blow trumpets (2). b. don't give in synagogue (2). c. don't give on the street (2). d. don't watch your own giving (3).	Give secretly (1, 4).
vv. 5, 6	Pray.	Don't pray to be seen by others like hypocrites: a. in synagogues (5). b. on street corners (5).	Pray privately: a. in your room (6). b. with door shut (6).
vv. 7-15	Pray.	Don't pray repetitiously like heathen: a. needlessly (7). b. with a lot of words (7).	Pray simply, briefly like the model I give you (9-13).
vv. 16-18	Fast.	Don't fast to be seen by others like hypocrites: a. by looking gloomy (16). b. by disfiguring your face (16). c. by showing your anointing (17).	Fast privately: Anoint face, then wash it (17).
vv. 19-24	Store up treasures in heaven	Don't store treasures on earth (19). Don't try to serve both God and money (24).	Solve the problem: a. it is not in money, b. it is in you—in your eye, not in what it sees (22, 23). Serve God alone (24).

Verses	Command	How not to obey it	How to obey it
vv. 25-34	Trust God to meet needs.	Don't focus your concerns and efforts on needs like pagans: a. food (25-32). b. clothing (25-32).	Focus efforts on: a. His kingdom. b. His righteousness. Focus on today's responsibilities.
Matt. 7:1-6	Judge properly.	Don't judge others a. when you have a bigger problem yourself (3, 4). b. when the other person is an unbeliever who won't appreciate it (6).	Judge only: a. when you judge as you want to be judged (2). b. when your own problem is solved (5). c. when the other is a brother (5, 6).
vv. 7-12	Ask.	Don't hesitate or doubt (implied).	Ask, seek, knock, knowing God gives as a good Father (11).
vv. 13, 14	Enter the way of life.	Don't enter by the wide gate (13).	Enter by the narrow gate (14).
vv. 15-20	Watch out for false prophets.	Don't follow those a. in sheep's clothing (15). b. whose fruit is bad (16-20).	Follow those with good fruit.
vv. 21-29	Be genuine and enter the kingdom.	Enter not by empty profession (21-23). Not by hearing alone (26, 27).	Enter by hearing, professing, and doing Christ's will (21, 24, 25).

Clearly, the Sermon on the Mount possesses an abundance of deliberate *how to*. Why have homileticians failed to notice this very obvious fact? Possibly because, unlike biblical counselors, they have not been aware of the importance of implementation in change. If you want your preaching to be effective, then, like Christ, be sure to give *how-to* help.[12]

While this chapter itself might have been developed into a book, and perhaps some day will be, even what has been shown here demonstrates fully enough the important role that an understanding of biblical counseling can play in preaching theory and practice.

12. Incidentally, notice that the Sermon on the Mount concludes powerfully with a story (vv. 24-27).

Class Assignment:

From your reading of at least one of the books on counseling mentioned in this chapter, write a paper indicating at least three ways in which biblical counseling principles or practices may be of help in preaching.

APPLICATION
OF TRUTH

Preachers and homileticians alike frequently speak about application. Typically, they talk about "applying" biblical truth to their congregations. But application itself is seldom defined and, what is of greater significance, the idea behind it is rarely discussed. Is it a biblical concept or not? And if so, what is its purpose? These are the basic questions to which I wish to draw your attention.

The idea of "application" does not quite fit the biblical picture. To speak of the preacher's obligation to apply the Scriptures to a congregation other than the one for whom it was originally written is not the way the Bible puts it. Listen carefully to Paul's words:

> Am I speaking from a human viewpoint, or does the law also say these things? It is written in Moses' law, "Don't muzzle an ox when it is threshing." It isn't about oxen that God is concerned, is it? Isn't He really speaking about us? It was written for us, because when the plowman plows and the thresher threshes he should do so in hope of having a share of the crop.

> Now these events happened as examples for us so that we might not desire evil things as they did. . . . Now these events happened to them as examples and were recorded as counsel for us who live at this late date in history (I Cor. 9:8-10; 10:6, 11).

Notice, Paul says nothing at all about *applying* a passage from the Old Testament to his readers. Rather, his words indicate that the Scripture was written for those he addresses as well as for its original recipients. He calls Old Testament passages "examples for *us* . . . ," says that they were "recorded as counsel for *us*" and even indicates that what was written had a deeper purpose to serve than those who received it originally might have imagined:

Isn't He [God] really speaking about *us?* It was written for *us*."

To say those words about the Bible— "It was written for *us*"—is to take a preaching view of scriptural revelation. Paul's conception of Scripture fits well the here-and-now preaching stance that I have discussed already. The words of the Bible are not merely the writings of Isaiah, John, or Paul; they are the words of the Spirit, who also knew what our situation today would be like. Though the Spirit addressed His Word to an immediate situation, with all of its color and ethos, He also designed that Word for us and for the whole church of all time. We may just as surely say of the New Testament what Paul said of the Old: "It was written for *us*."

This view of the Scriptures runs throughout the New Testament. Consider Romans 4:23, 24a:

The words, "it was counted to him," weren't written for his sake *alone*, but *also* for *our* sake.

The words, "weren't written for his [Abraham's] sake alone," make it perfectly plain that God wrote for *both*, not just for the one or the other. "Also" is inclusive of both, and "for *our* sake" clearly specifies those of Paul's day as parties to God's written promise. There is no place for application by Paul to his readers; God Himself addressed His message equally to them. God does the applying.

Again, in Romans 15:4, Paul explained,

Whatever was written before was written for *our* instruction.

God was teaching *us* when He taught the Old Testament saints, Paul claimed. Again, application is not in view; rather, a view of the whole

Bible ("'whatever was written before'') as valid for the church of all time is set forth.

When this biblical view of the Bible is adopted, therefore, you will soon find that your preparation for preaching is not so much a matter of finding ways in which *you* must "apply" passages to your congregation as it is a matter of discovering how God Himself has already applied His Word to it. Again, Paul's view emphasizes the *telic* thrust of each preaching portion. It is God's task to apply the Scriptures, then, not yours. Your task is to discover what that application is and to translate the passage into contemporary forms.

To speak of the preacher "applying" the truth of the Scripture to a congregation, therefore, is to miss the mark, if by that is meant *you* are the one who determines the application. The truth, *when given,* was already applied to the whole church by God, who Himself determined its application. It is not as though it is necessary for you to *find* some way to apply it. You must apply truth as God does.

What am I saying? My point is simply this: God did not reveal truth in the abstract. Whenever He gave new revelation, He did so within the context of the lives of His people. The truth was revealed *into* a situation *to which it applied.* Just as we have no right using a preaching portion for purposes other than that which God intended it to serve, neither do we have the option to "apply" it, as many do, to any and all circumstances that we may choose. Therefore, to preach the Bible faithfully in our time, we must find the *equivalent* to the original circumstance or situation to which God then (and now) applied the warning, the promise, the principle, or the command.

All of this is to say that because, as I Corinthians 10:11, 13 proves, basically people and their problems (as well as God's solutions to them) remain the same in all generations, there *is* a circumstance today that corresponds to the original one, to which God *also* directed His Word. When God delivered His message then, He did not direct it only toward the people to whom it was given originally but toward the church in all ages to follow. At bottom, scraping off all the superficial, local, and time-bound features of the past *and* of the present circumstance or the situation, in one way or another you will find persons struggling with issues and practices having to do with love to God and love to their neighbors. The first and fundamental point to be made, then, is that God Himself has determined the application of His Word to your church.

If you come to believe and understand this, you will want to convince your congregation, as Paul sought to convince the Romans and the Corinthians, that God's Word was written to and applies to *them,* not only to others long ago and far away. He tells the Corinthians that basically they experience nothing different from what the Israelites experienced so many years before:

> Now these events happened to them as examples and were recorded as counsel for us who live at this late date in history. . . . No trial has taken hold of you except that which other people have experienced; but God is faithful Who will not allow you to be tried beyond what you are able to bear, but rather, will provide together with the trial the way out so that you may be able to endure it (I Cor. 10:11, 13).

In I Corinthians 10:11, Paul insists that even though the Corinthians were living at a much later date in history, nonetheless, what was written long before was written as *counsel* for *them.* In verses 6-10 there is an example of just how Paul discovered and used God's present application of His Word to the Corinthians:

> Now these events happened as examples for us so that we might not desire evil things as they did. Don't become idolaters as some of them were; as it is written: "The people sat down to drink and they stood up to revel." We must not commit sexual sins as some of them did, and twenty-three thousand fell in a single day. Neither should we test the Lord as some of them did and were destroyed by snakes. Nor should you grumble as some of them did and were destroyed by the destroyer.

Note the similarity of the circumstances that Paul saw as it is indicated in the recurring words, "as some of them."

Again and again this emphasis appears. Consider Galatians 3:29, for example:

> And if you are of Christ, then you are Abraham's seed, heirs in keeping with the promise.

Notice how Paul maintains that the promise made to Abraham is a promise the benefits of which his readers (and with him, *we* must also say Christian congregations today) may enter into by faith in Christ. Peter also treats the promises made to Israel as promises to the New Testament church:

> But you have become a chosen race, a kingly priesthood, a holy nation, a people who belong to Someone, so that you may declare the virtues of the One Who called you out of darkness into His amazing light (I Pet. 2:9).

And the writer of Hebrews sketched the same continuity of God's promised blessings when he wrote:

> And these all received good testimony because of their faith; yet they didn't receive what was promised because God had something better in sight for us. So then they couldn't be made perfect without us (Heb. 11:39, 40).

And this same writer affirmed God's love to the suffering church to which he was writing by declaring that a passage in the Book of Proverbs was written to *them:*

> . . . in your struggle against sin you haven't yet had to resist to the point of shedding your blood.
>
> Now, have you forgotten the encouragement that reasons with you as sons?—"My son, don't think lightly of the Lord's discipline, and don't give up when He corrects you. The Lord disciplines those whom He loves, and whips every son that He receives (Heb. 12:4-6).

In the preface to the quotation notice his words, ". . . the encouragement that reasons with *you* as sons . . ." (5a).[1] Christ also treated the Scriptures in this way:

> And He said to them, "Isaiah properly prophesied about you hypocrites! As it is written: 'These people honor Me with the lips but their hearts are far away from Me. They worship me in vain, teaching human commandments as their teachings.' You let go of God's commandments and hold on to human traditions!" (Mark 7:6-8).

1. Cf. also Heb. 6:13-18 (esp. v. 18) and Heb. 13:5.

Don't miss His words, "Isaiah properly prophesied about *you* . . ." (6ª).[2]

Manifestly, these passages demonstrate the point that I have been making: the New Testament writers considered the Old Testament to have been written to the whole church of all time; they knew, therefore, that God Himself was applying His Word. It was their task to uncover, explain, and impress this application upon their congregations. They must apply the truth as God Himself has. Paul summarized it well when he wrote:

> Whatever was written before was written for our instruction, that by the endurance and the encouragement that the Scriptures give us we may have hope (Rom. 15:4).

I do wish only to add one consideration: while God already has applied His message, the circumstance in the original form into which God spoke His Word will have to be dissected carefully to separate the basic and ongoing factors from those which are temporary and incidental. This constitutes the "translation" of which I am speaking. Here is precisely where many preachers go wrong. Discovering similarities is not enough; the similarities that count are those which are basic, not those which are secondary. To find a correlation between superficial factors is to allow one's self to be deflected from the *telic* thrust of a preaching portion to something that was not intended at all. What, then, is constant?

In Hebrews 4:11, the writer speaks of "*the same pattern* of disobedience." The similarity had to do with lack of "faith" and refusal to "obey" the truth (vv. 2, 6), not with any secondary factors in the circumstance. Again, in I Corinthians 10:6, 11 we read of the "pattern" or "example": "idolatry" (v. 7), "sexual sin" (v. 8), "testing the Lord" (v. 9), and "grumbling" (v. 10). It is not the *manner* of idolatry that is of importance, nor the circumstances *connected with* the sexual sin, nor the *way* in which the Lord was tested, nor *the matters about which* the people grumbled that were of significance, but the idolatry, sexual sin, testing, and the grumbling in these

2. Cf. Matt. 15:7-9; John 12:40, 41.

situations that were the constant factors to which the biblical accounts speak in all ages. So, too, Paul observes that the principle in I Corinthians 9:9, 10 is broader, greater, and more universal than the original statement of it in the particular case in which it was applied to oxen. The task, then, is to find the constant, or the basic thrust in each circumstance to which God's authoritative Word speaks. Because this is so important a matter, an entire book must be devoted to it sometime in the future. But for now, let us turn to the vital matter of implementation of biblical truth.

Class Assignment:

Demonstrate from five preaching portions not mentioned in this chapter how God applies His message today.

19

THE PURPOSE OF
IMPLEMENTATION

In a previous chapter I demonstrated the importance of the implementation of biblical truth in edificational preaching from the Sermon on the Mount. In that sermon Jesus implemented every command by explicit *how to* (and how not to) instructions. It would be wise not only to follow His lead but also to discuss how that may be done.

Typically, Bible-believing preachers have implemented neither positively nor negatively, by *how* or how *not* to. They have been good at telling congregations what to do, but notoriously poor at telling them how to do it. A preacher will get up in the pulpit and say, "Don't just read your Bible; study it!" So far, so good. But what happens when John Greene goes home and tries to do so? He is full of enthusiastic conviction—but totally void of any new ways and means to do so. So, he turns to Genesis 1:1 and with great intensity starts to . . . *read!* He can do nothing different; he doesn't know how. By the time he arrives at the so-and-so-begat-so-and-so passages on Wednesday, he realizes he is doing nothing but what he has been doing all along—and quits, discouraged. This is the umpteenth time he has attempted to "really study the Bible." Each time he meant it; he always began with enthusiasm, but each time he ended poorly—in discouragement! This time, as he closes the Book, he says to himself, "Well, I guess Paul could do it, but I'm not Paul!"

What has been going wrong? John needs *how to*. If his pastor had recognized this fact and if, when he shouted "Don't just read your Bible; study it!" he had continued, saying, ". . . and if you don't know *how* to study your Bible, be here tonight one hour before the evening service for the first of 12 lessons on "How to Study the Bible," John would have been O.K. But as it is, he has good intentions—even tries again, but to no avail. This is the last attempt; finally John has given up for good. Another preaching casualty has bit the dust! John will join the ranks of that great band of church goers who, because they have given up, become deadwood in the pews, there to remain until some preacher—if any ever does—comes to resurrect him from among the dead by preaching *how to*.

It was while doing counseling that I discovered the need for and importance of *how to*. When I began to help people lay plans to do whatever the Scriptures said they must do, and began to suggest ways and means for doing it, I noticed that many of them came alive. So, I began to preach with *how to* and again noticed that the same phenomenon occurred. I knew I was onto something then. But it wasn't until I made a study of the Sermon on the Mount that it became crystal clear that providing direction is a part of good biblical preaching.

What happens to all the John Greenes is this: they try and fail; then they try and fail again; then, once more—the same thing happens. This goes on and on until they finally give up for good. They shouldn't, it is true. They should persevere until they succeed. They should knock on their pastors' doors until they can persuade their pastors to teach them *how* to do whatever it is they are failing to do; but as sinners they don't persevere. That is why you, as a preacher, must do something yourself to help them. You must provide the *how to* that will enable them to implement the thrust of your sermon.

In doing so, it is important to distinguish plainly between (1) biblical commands, principles, practices, and biblically directed *how to*[1] on the one hand and (2) suggested, biblically derived *how to* devised by the preacher.

When the Scriptures do not spell out the how-to, as they sometimes do, they leave us on our own to devise ways and means of implementing the principles and general practices that they require. Counselors always must distinguish between the inspired principle and the suggested, but uninspired, implementation of it. There may be more than one way of implementing the same principle. The *principle* must be *insisted* upon; the specific way of *implementation* may only be *suggested*. All methods for implementing biblical principles should grow out of those (and other biblical) principles and be appropriate to them at every point. That is to say, even the suggestions that a preacher makes must be able to be justified as *derived* from biblical principles and totally in accord with them.

While I cannot go into details about how to do *how to* in this chapter, I would refer you to the discussion of the subject in my book, *Insight and Creativity in Christian Counseling*. A certain amount of creativity is required to devise adequate implementation for biblical directives. In that book I have set forth a method (i.e., some pertinent *how to*) for developing and employing creative *how to* (what I have said there about *how to* in counseling is equally useful for preaching). However, in this chapter I wish to discuss more fundamental issues about implementation in relation to preaching.

Let us say you are about to preach the last of a series of four sermons on the four steps of biblically caused change listed in II Timothy 3:16:

1. teaching,
2. conviction,
3. correction,
4. and disciplined training in righteousness.

You are preparing a message on step 4. As you study the passage, among other things you ask, "What is the responsibility of the person in the pew to use the Bible for disciplined training in righteousness?"

---

1. This is *how to* that is spelled out in the Bible itself.

Your concern is not how *you* may use it to help bring about discipline—that you know. Rather, at this point in your preparation your concern is

1. What is my member's role in this process, and
2. how do I teach him to implement his role?

First, you see immediately that there is no direct answer to either question in the context. You will have to determine the best response to the first question from a comparison of the phrase with other biblical teaching on discipline and what it is designed to produce: righteousness (i.e., godly life patterns). Let us say you conclude from Ephesians 4, Colossians 3, Philippians 4:9, etc., that it will take regular practice in obedience to biblical principles in order to come to the place where your listener can be said to "walk in the truth," as John puts it, or to have "disciplined himself toward godliness," as Paul says elsewhere. Since the preaching portion itself says nothing about "putting on," "disciplining one's self toward," or "walking" in any particular practice, but speaks only generally of "righteousness," you conclude that it is the process itself on which the Holy Spirit has focused His attention. Moreover, the passage is not addressed to the members of the flock, but to the shepherd, who must guide them into the disciplined paths of righteousness for Christ's Name sake. The purpose of the passage is to urge the shepherd to make full use of the all-sufficient Scriptures to effect change in the lives of his sheep, one crucial aspect of which is to train them in righteous biblical patterns of living. Once the shepherd has "taught" them God's standards, once he has brought them to "conviction" of their failure to measure up to those standards, and once he has helped them to "correct" their sinful ways through confession of sin and forgiveness in repentance—all by the Word—*then* he is to train them, in a disciplined way, in the biblical alternatives to their former sinful patterns. Presuming that the sheep have been progressing well through the first three steps, what does he do about the fourth?

Clearly, the *sheep* are to understand and accept the biblical "teaching" unfolded and impressed upon them through the shepherd's preaching and counseling. The shepherd cannot understand or accept for them—in their place. His task is to explain the teaching to them. Moreover, the *sheep* have to sense the guilt of conviction and repent of their sin; again, the shepherd's task is to use the Word effectively, in the power of the Spirit, to bring this about. But he cannot repent for them; he can help them to implement the truth. Though he cannot "practice" ways of righteousness for them, he can help them in their training in God's righteous ways.

So, in preaching from this passage, the shepherd can set forth the training dynamic for his flock, he can explain his role and theirs, he can call on them to avail themselves of his shepherdly direction, guidance, and supervision while in training. He can run through the process in terms of some specific cases (a liar becoming a truth teller, a sluggard becoming an industrious person, a vengeful person becoming one who does good to those who wrong him) and in each case demonstrate what part he can play, by the proper use of the Scriptures, in bringing about their new lifestyles.

But all of that seems so general. How does he implement it? He may suggest something like this:

> Now, if, after attempting to put the new ways into effect on your own, you discover that you seem not to be succeeding, *please call me immediately*. At that point I shall gladly sit down with you and go over the whole terrain to see if there are any flaws in what you are doing that might be corrected. On the other hand, if the problem is discipline itself, and you need help in this, I shall either supervise you myself or help you to work out a plan to get the supervision you require. Either way, don't go on struggling, stumbling about and failing when God has provided me as a Timothy for you to help you bring the Bible to bear on your life with power and effectiveness. Don't say, "Oh, I don't want to bother the preacher." That kind of phone call is no bother! This is what I *should* be doing, what I *want* to be doing. Call today, if necessary. Don't put it off; call just as soon as you recognize your need.

What you have just been reading has double impact: it is an offer of assistance in devising implementation that, itself, spells out a way of implementation for obtaining it.

Now, let us suppose the suggested implementation ("Call me today") gets results: Mildred calls. An appointment is made, and a problem is identified. Counseling will result, in which, ultimately, a plan is developed and put into effect. Perhaps it is quite successful; Mildred is grateful. Then, later, the preacher phones Mildred and says:

"Mildred, during those six weeks that we counseled together you came a long way and learned much. Did you find the program we followed helpful?"

"Oh yes, pastor."

"Well, I'm glad. But I suspect that the training plan that you have found helpful in solving your temper problem might also be useful to a number of other persons in the congregation. I am sure you aren't the only one who has had difficulty with her temper. I want you to know that I intend to preach soon about this aspect of anger, and I shall be suggesting that others use a program similar to the one you used. Now, I want you to feel perfectly at ease when I do. Though you will hear some things that are quite familiar to you, I don't intend to mention you or anything about your situation. But you will recognize the problem and parts of the plan, so I thought I should let you know ahead of time, so you would be ready for it."

"Well, I appreciate your telling me so. I might have had an initial shock otherwise, wondering whether what you were going to say would involve me!"

"Have no fear. But certainly, if God blessed you so much through what was done, it would be important to share the same basic information with others, don't you think?"

"I sure do. In fact, I wouldn't mind at all if you did mention what happened in my case, so long as you don't identify *me*."

"Thanks. With your permission I might do so."[2]

---

2. If he does, of course, (1) he will be careful to say nothing that might betray who it was he is mentioning, and (2) he will make it clear that what he does say is only by permission.

"Thank *you*. I'll really be waiting for *that* sermon."[3]

Now, in conclusion, let us examine what we have discovered about implementation by asking, "What is the *purpose* of implementation?"

In reply, let me confess that, like many other chapters in this book, this is an unusual one. Homileticians write about application (usually wrongly), but they do not even write about implementation. So why did I? Because I have found that Jesus firmly affixed enabling directions to His commands. He did so for a purpose; Jesus does nothing aimlessly. His purpose emerges at the conclusion of the Sermon on the Mount:

> "Not everyone who says to Me, 'Lord, Lord,' will enter into the empire from the heavens, but only the one who does the will of My Father Who is in the heavens. . . . So then, whoever hears these words of Mine and does them may be compared to a wise man who built his house on the rock" (Matt. 7:21, 24).

It is evident from these two verses that Jesus expected His disciples not merely to hear His words, nor even to hear them with approval, but also to *obey* them (cf. also Luke 6:47). He *ends* on that note. And remember, it is in the conclusion that you will find the purpose of a sermon if it is well constructed. The final story of the two houses (a good example of a story conclusion) makes the point most vividly. He aimed at action: *"do* them," He said. He preached for results. And there would be no one who heard that message who could have the slightest excuse for not doing as He said. The double implementation, with both its *how to* and its how *not* to, precluded that. But of greater importance, all who desired to obey would know how; they would not be frustrated by their own ineptness or confusion. Not only were the commands clear, but how to obey them was spelled out just as clearly. For the same purposes, you too must learn to use implementation in your sermons.

---

3. Incidentally, notice how the preacher solved the problem of using cases in preaching by using case *programs* and case *procedures*. And, note well, his consideration in calling Mildred led to permission to use even more.

Class Assignments:

1. Discover three sermons that contain implementation.
2. If you cannot find that many, add your own implementation to those you find. Write out your final work and be ready to present it in class.

PREACHING
CHRIST

It is easy to become moralistic when preaching. While there is nothing wrong with preaching morality, in contrast, moral*ism* is legalistic, ignores the grace of God, and replaces the work of Christ with self-help. In *The Christian Counselor's Wordbook,* I wrote,

> Legalists assume that one can obey God's commandments (1) without salvation and/or (2) in his own strength. Both ideas are false and can be very detrimental in counseling. Prayerful action . . . in the power of the Spirit is required for change to be biblical; all change that pleases God is the fruit (result of the work) of the Spirit.

> There is no merit in keeping God's commandments (Luke 17:10), nor does He accept outward conformity alone. Rather, He demands inner change of the heart . . . as the source and power behind any outer change.

> Counselees often come with legalistic ideas about how to get out of their dilemmas and will attempt to follow biblical principles *as a gimmick.* Counselors must warn them against such ideas, call them to repentance where it is required, and make it plain that above all else is the necessity of doing what must be done to

please God. One's relationship to God is basic to all else that is attempted in counseling.[1]

What applies to counseling applies equally to preaching.

If you preach a sermon that would be acceptable to the members of a Jewish synagogue or to a Unitarian congregation, there is something radically wrong with it. Preaching, when truly Christian, is *distinctive*. And what makes it distinctive is the all-pervading presence of a saving and sanctifying Christ. Jesus Christ must be at the heart of every sermon you preach. That is just as true of edificational preaching as it is of evangelistic preaching.

But, while edificational preaching always must be evangelical, it must not become simply evangelistic. An evangelistic sermon is a sermon in which the major thrust is to proclaim the gospel with the intent of calling unbelievers to faith in Christ. That is a worthy purpose and has its place, but my concern here is to discuss the place of Christ in edificational preaching. Edificational preaching is no longer edificational in purpose if the purpose of the sermon becomes evangelistic instead.

However, edificational preaching always must be evangelical; that is what makes it moral rather than moralistic, and what causes it to be unacceptable in a synagogue, in a mosque, or to a Unitarian congregation. By evangelical, I mean that the import of Christ's death and resurrection—His substitutionary, penal death and bodily resurrection—on the subject under consideration is made clear in the sermon. You must not exhort your congregation to do whatever the Bible requires of them as though they could fulfil those requirements on their own, but only as a consequence of the saving power of the cross and the indwelling, sanctifying power and presence of Christ in the person of the Holy Spirit. All edificational preaching, to be Christian, must fully take into consideration God's grace in salvation and in sanctification.

Today, one of the greatest threats to evangelical preaching comes from the invasion of the church by the Adler-Maslow, etc., self-

1. Jay E. Adams, *The Christian Counselor's Wordbook* (Phillipsburg, N.J.), pp. 60-61.

image, self-worth dogmas. Passage after passage in the Bible has been distorted in order to conform to these teachings, with the result that you end up preaching man and his supposed worth rather than Christ. Sometimes that "worth" has been seen as intrinsic, sometimes it has been considered to be the result of salvation.

Certainly the message of the entire Book of Ecclesiastes is that there is no intrinsic worth in man; there is nothing but emptiness, worthlessness. All that makes sense, in the *end* ("the *conclusion* of the whole matter," Eccles. 12:14) is that unless one "fears God" (is justified) and "keeps His commandments" (grows in sanctification), all is vanity. Indeed, man is as empty and worthless as a shadow or a moth (Ps. 39:6, 11); he is utterly empty (Ps. 39:5, 11)—of absolutely no weight (Ps. 62:9) apart from Christ. Intrinsically, then, man has no self-worth. Whatever self-worth he pretends to discover in himself is only illusory and, in the end, as Ecclesiastes says, vanishes. Anything worthwhile arises from salvation (fearing God) and sanctification (keeping His commandments). So, the idea of intrinsic self-worth must be dismissed.

Most Christians, instead, have developed the idea of a self-worth in Christ that should be the basis for every believer having a good self-image. The notion is that without a good self-image we will accomplish little for Christ. Because in Christ we are (rightly) considered to be all that He is, this fact is supposed to provide for us a good self-image—simply by *recognizing* the fact, or by telling ourselves so often enough. This unbiblical nonsense has been accepted even by theologians, who ought to know better (cf. A. A. Hoekema's, *A Christian Looks At Himself*). With a naivete that is culpable, we are led to believe that what Christ has done for us should give us a good self-image. Of course, it does nothing of the sort.

First of all, the Bible says nothing about the need for a good self-image. It certainly doesn't condition our ability to obey God on a sense of self-worth! And nowhere are we even commanded to improve our self-image. None of this is scriptural.

"But what of the passages that speak about 'considering' yourself 'dead to sin' and 'alive to God,' etc.?" you may ask.

I am glad you brought up Romans 6. You could add Ephesians 4 and Colossians 3 as well. But in none of these passages is there the slightest hint that we are told that in Christ we have "put on" the "new person," or that we are "raised together" and seated in the heavenlies with Him *in order to* give us a sense of self-worth or a good self-image. To represent (*mis*represent) them as *teaching* such things about self-worth is not only to miss the *telic* thrust of these passages, it is to import pagan psychological ideas into the Bible.

What do these passages teach? Every such passage, without exception, is a passage stressing one's potential in Christ. The positional factor (i.e., what we are in Christ) is mentioned only as an argument to encourage us to become what we should. Listen to Colossians 3:1: "If you were raised together with Christ [the positional truth] seek the things that are above, where Christ is seated at God's right hand [the unrealized potential to be attained]." Throughout that chapter and the parallel passages in Ephesians 4, the same argument is pressed: Become in your daily living (since you are not) what you already are (positionally) in Christ. Live up to your potential in Christ. In Romans 6 the very same case is true—we are to count ourselves dead to sin and alive to God (positionally) in Christ, so that we may live no longer in sin but in righteousness day by day. Because of what Christ has done for us we are counted righteous by God, and we now have the potential to become in everyday living what we already are counted to be; so realize your potential. That is the argument. There isn't a whisper of anything about developing a good self-image in *any* of these passages.

It is not because these passages teach the pursuit of self-worth that they have been used for that purpose. Reading them, no one would ever imagine that they did (indeed, prior to the self-image craze in psychology, no one ever did). But, because a psychological view has been accepted, Christians who bought it have been searching for biblical support. These passages have been seized upon to lend that support when, in fact, they do no such thing.

Actually, the more one recognizes how high his position is in Christ, and the great potential that regeneration has afforded him to grow toward that position, the *worse* his self-image is likely to be if he is not actually moving toward it as he should. The more he recognizes the enormous disparity that exists between his realized position in Christ and his largely unrealized potential in daily living, the more he should repent. In fact, as has often been observed, throughout his ministry Paul himself seemed to grow in recognition of his own sin.

In contrast to all that psychologizers of the Bible teach, the truth is that the Scriptures tell us *not* to pursue self:

> Then He said to all of them, ''If anybody wants to come after Me, he must deny himself and take up his cross daily and follow Me. This is true because whoever wants to save his life will lose it, and whoever loses his life for My sake will save it. What does it profit a person if he gains the whole world and loses or forfeits himself? Whoever is ashamed of Me and My words, of him the Son of Man will be ashamed when He comes with His glory and with the glory of the Father and of the holy angels . . .'' (Luke 9:23-26).

The self is to be ''denied'' and ''lost.'' In that way alone—not by the pursuit of a good self-image—will the self ultimately be found. A good self-image, like happiness, peace, and joy, is not to be found by seeking it. All these things are by-products that cannot be obtained directly. They come *when something else* is realized. In this case, the self is *saved* when it is *lost* for Christ and for the sake of His gospel (cf. Mark 8:35). A person cannot expect to have a good self-image until he becomes a good self. Pumping up a self-image doesn't work.

Now, what has all this to do with preaching Christ, and preaching evangelically? Just this: it is a prime example of how the Bible is misused today to exalt humanity rather than Christ. To preach the passages that I have mentioned as they were intended to be preached, Christ must be exalted as the One who not only has effected our justification (the declaration by God that in Him we are counted perfect), but also has made sanctification possible by sending His Spirit to enable us to understand God's revealed will and to empower us to do it. What Christ has done is put quite forcefully by Peter in a passage whose import is similar to that in Romans 6:

> Therefore, since Christ has suffered in the flesh, arm yourselves

also with that thought, because whoever has suffered in the flesh has come to a parting of the ways with sin. As a result, it is now possible to live the remainder of your time in the flesh no longer following human desires, but following the will of God (I Pet. 4:1, 2).

When we get the proper view of our justification as a ''parting of ways with sin'' (in Christ), we may also see clearly that it is ''now possible to live the remainder of our lives in the flesh no longer following human desires, but following the will of God.'' Again, justification leads to the possibilities of sanctification. But if we don't grow, if we ''continue in sin,'' if we fail to ''seek those things that are above,'' how can we expect to have a good self-image?

A good self-image comes not merely from acknowledging what we are in Christ, as the psychologizers suppose, but also from closing the gap between what we are in Christ and what we should become in our daily living. That is to say, it comes not only from justification, but also as a by-product of progress in sanctification.

And sanctification, as we have seen, is the work of Christ, the Spirit, in us. So, in preaching Christ we must preach Him as the One who made our acceptance with God a reality by His death on the cross and as the One whose continued work in us conforms us more and more to the standards of the Word. In short, to preach Christ is to preach both what He has done and what He is doing.

That is the way that the New Testament writers preached: they found Him in all the Scriptures. We must do the same. That is what He, Himself, taught us to do when he ''opened'' the Scriptures to the disciples on the road to Emmaus and

> beginning with Moses, He went through all the prophets and explained to them in all the Scriptures the things that concerned Himself (Luke 24:27).

Christ is in ''all the Scriptures,'' and you must find Him there. He is there, making all possible by His saving and sanctifying power. Everything must be preached that way. When it is, members of the congregation will be heard to echo the disciples' words: ''Didn't our hearts burn within us . . . as He opened the Scriptures to us?" (Luke 24:32).

So, when you preach about giving, preach it in the light of Christ's matchless gift as Paul did (II Cor. 9:15). When you preach about a husband's love for his wife, preach it in the light of the love of the cross (Eph. 5:25). When you preach about work, preach it as service to Christ (Col. 3). All you say and do in preaching must be related to Him; it must be related to His saving and His sanctifying work. When you do this, legalism will vanish, hypocritical, outward conformity to biblical standards used as a gimmick will be countered, and the pursuit of human self-worth will be scrapped in favor of a desire to please Him. Obedience will not be mere duty; it will have about it a doxological ring.

So, then, preach Christ. Preach Him plainly and gratefully, and you will not be tempted to preach about man and his pretended powers and dignity. Preach Christ in all the Scriptures: He is the subject matter of the whole Bible. He is there. Until you have found Him in your preaching portion, you are not ready to preach. Search Him out; preach *Him*—and hearts will burn.

Class Assignment:

> Choose three preaching portions not directly mentioning Jesus Christ and determine how Christ might be preached from them. Discuss this in a three-page paper.

21

DELIVERY
AND PURPOSE

In this book I have attempted not to replicate that which may be found already in my book, *Pulpit Speech*. There I have discussed delivery—the use of voice and body—in great depth. There is little to add. So, it is not because I believe delivery is unimportant that I include so little about it here; no. Quite the contrary. Because I knew it was so important, I have already written extensively on the subject in the previously published volume.

What more can be said here?

First, I should mention the sad failure of many Bible-believing men to take the trouble to think about and work on delivery. Because of this failure, much truth, in turn, has failed to have its impact.

There are four principal factors that converge as joint carriers of the preacher's message: language, order, voice, and body. Delivery—the use of voice and body—comprises fully one half of these. Therefore delivery ought not to be given the short shrift that so many conservative preachers give it.

Great *content*, set forth in the most logical *order* and with the exact *words* appropriate to it, can be grossly distorted, or even totally destroyed, by careless, lackluster, inappropriate, or conflicting delivery. There is matter in manner.

Like it or not, your attitude (or an attitude presumed by the congregation to be yours) toward the biblical content that you proclaim is also proclaimed—most fully by your voice and body. Your words may declare that the truth you are expounding is of great importance, but your manner may say otherwise. Tragically, often when you really do think something is vitally important, etc., your frozen, wooden—perhaps fearful—delivery unintentionally (and probably unknowingly) may say just the opposite. Many otherwise potentially excellent messages have been ruined by poor delivery.

So, what you must work on is:

1. Not allowing personal practices, habits, patterns, mannerisms, and fear in the use of voice and body to get in the way of the message;
2. Developing a flexibility in the use of voice and body broad enough to match the wide spectrum of biblical teaching;
3. Adopting a willingness to allow biblical content to determine how your voice and body will respond, regardless of what that requires.

These are the three areas in which you should concentrate your efforts. For help on each, see *Pulpit Speech*. You will notice that among them there is no effort to set forth some standard *form* for good delivery. There is no such form. Problems occur whenever someone attempts to standardize. Rather, the standard delivery to be adopted is the one that grows out of and is appropriate to the content at any given point.

Delivery will take care of itself to a great extent when you allow yourself to feel, or experience, the emotional impact of what the content is teaching. When you are willing to *relive* the event about which you are speaking, or *prelive* it in your imagination if it is something not previously experienced, rather than *reporting* (or *pre-reporting*) it, you will find that delivery follows and flows from content very naturally.

The point is that either your delivery will affect the content (adversely), or the content will affect the delivery (helpfully). Because the two are so tightly intertwined, there is no possibility of avoiding influence—in one direction or the other. The key thing, then, is to be assured the content to be conveyed always has the upper hand.

This philosophy of delivery conforms to the fundamental point I have been making all along: that *it is the purpose of the passage that must be uppermost.* This is true just as well for delivery as for anything else: God's purpose must control all. All error in preaching, in one way or another, stems from placing our own purposes or personalities above God's.

The Bible exalts Christ, not men. He should be seen in a sermon, not the preacher who becomes more visible than Christ because of his unbecoming delivery. In every respect, including his use of delivery, the preacher must put Christ first.

This point becomes clear in the interplay between content and delivery at every stage. If God's purpose in a passage is solemn and grim, your delivery must not make light of it, either intentionally or unintentionally. If God's purpose is a joyful one, you dare not grind that through a personality grid that is so inflexible and insensitive that the message comes out drab or even solemn. In short, you must allow even your personality to be changed, if and when necessary, by God's truth. A minister of the Word, when faithful to his calling, in every way becomes just *that*—one in whom the Word has absolute sway, even to the point of great personality change in him. The delivery you should seek, then, is a delivery that is formed, informed, and influenced by God's truth. The best preacher is the one who allows his voice and body to become a well-tuned instrument in the hands of the Holy Spirit. He is willing, therefore, to be stretched, squeezed, and otherwise altered to meet every demand necessary to preaching the *whole* counsel of God. With those words, I shall close my remarks on delivery.

22

CONCLUSION

A rare thing happened the other day—I heard a good sermon. Let me briefly analyze it for you, noting some of the factors that made it good.

First, it was *preaching;* it was not a string of stories or a stodgy lecture. By that I mean, from start to finish, the sermon was directed to *us*. We were involved from the outset. The truth of the passage was presented as God's message to *us,* not only to the members of a church long ago and far away in biblical times. God came alive as someone living, ruling, caring *now*—for *us*. The preacher made us concerned, and kept us concerned, about *our* families, *our* church, *our* community.

Next, what I heard was *biblical* preaching. What was preached was not an essay on some truth, not the ideas of politicians, media personalities, philosophers, theologians or his own opinions, but what *God* said to us in Paul's letter. Not only did the preacher tell us what the preaching portion means, but he even showed us just how every point that he made comes from the passage. Because he did so, we were able to evaluate for ourselves whether the preacher's conclusions about the text were accurate. Significantly, it was apparent that he had done his homework and that what he told us made sense. And, I believe others in the congregation, if asked, would agree with me that what he said about the text was accurate. He satisfied us that he was preaching what Paul had said. We went away understanding the passage and how everything in the sermon flowed from it. Consequently, we listened to his exhortations about our lives, not as the opinions of a man, but as a word from God to us. He preached, and his preaching was received, with an authority appropriate to the sort of message that it was. We left knowing that we had heard a proclamation from God.

Again, the sermon was *interesting*. The preacher did not cook the juice out of the passage, leaving hard, dry, burned-over abstract teaching. Nor did he serve it to us as a raw, bloody, uncooked chunk of meat. Like a fine chef, he knew just how to handle the passage, cooking it to a turn, garnishing and accenting it so that what he served was the text in full flavor. Its own nutritious juices were preserved, and where delicate nuances otherwise might be missed, he seasoned it with illustrations that brought them out. As he delivered it, the sermon sizzled!

Moreover, the sermon was well *organized*. There were points, sturdy as steel, undergirding the whole, arranged in logical order. But the points did not protrude; he did not bore us with unnecessary firstlies, secondlies, and thirdlies; he avoided details that added nothing to the central idea of the message, and—believe it or not—he did not bother us with distracting, forced alliteration. His entire focus in the sermon was on the intent of the Holy Spirit in the text. He kept moving ahead, avoiding all meaningless prefacing and repetition, instead skillfully thrusting each point straight into our hearts! And the sermon was evangelical; he preached the gospel—clearly—but it was not merely another evangelical sermon. There was meat for believers. Yet that meat had been marinated in the truth of the cross.

Now, I know that you will find it difficult to believe me when I tell you that, on top of everything else, that sermon was *practical*. Yes, it really was! It was carefully adapted to the particular congregation to which it was preached. And the preacher persisted in telling us not only *what* to do but *how* to do it. And sometimes, like his Lord in the

Sermon on the Mount, he also told us how not to do it. It was plain that he had spent time thinking about what biblical principles mean in everyday living and had worked out biblically derived applications and implementations of each one. That was preaching with purpose!

What a sermon it was! You don't hear many like it today. Indeed, because of this fact, you may wonder where it was preached and who preached it. You may ask, ''Are cassette tapes available?'' The answer is no. But I can tell you where I heard it—it was in a reverie while sitting in the Montreal airport that I heard that sermon, and the only record of it is the one that I am now sketching for you enroute to Moncton. But, is it doomed to remain merely a bare record, hidden away from the people of God in a homiletic textbook sitting on your shelf? Why should it? Why don't you bring it to life? Why don't you preach it this Sunday to *your* congregation? Then, if you and scores of other preachers like you, do so, thousands of people throughout the land will truly be able to say, ''I heard a good sermon today!''

INDEX